THE SPIRIT OF ENGLISH HISTORY

THE SPIRIT
OF ENGLISH HISTORY

A. L. ROWSE

FELLOW OF ALL SOULS COLLEGE, OXFORD

WITH SIX MAPS

OXFORD UNIVERSITY PRESS
NEW YORK
1945

FIRST PUBLISHED IN GREAT BRITAIN IN 1943

This book was written at the request of the
British Council and is published by arrange-
ment with them, but the views expressed are
the author's and are not necessarily those of
the Council.

PRINTED IN THE UNITED STATES OF AMERICA

Preface

IN writing this book I have had two aims mainly in mind. First, to make the story of our people *intelligible*. That is, to make clear the circumstances of environment and stock, the factors and forces which have made our history what it is. Secondly, I have tried as far as possible within the very restricted confines at my disposal to include everything that is really *essential* to the understanding of that story.

I should like here to acknowledge my great indebtedness to that masterpiece of historical writing, G. M. Trevelyan's *History of England;* all the more so because my own approach is somewhat different, and on various questions I have taken another line. I am indebted to Mr. K. B. McFarlane, Vice-President of Magdalen College, Oxford, for reading my medieval chapters for me; to Dr. Charles Singer for kindly helping me with the sections on British scientists. My chief obligation is to Mr. Jack Simmons of Christ Church, who has gone through the whole book with me, and whose judgment and historical knowledge have saved me from many errors.

A. L. ROWSE

ALL SOULS COLLEGE,
    OXFORD

Contents

Maps

THE SPIRIT OF ENGLISH HISTORY

I. The Island and the People

ENGLISH history is the story of a people of mixed stock, mainly Teuton and Celtic, inhabiting an island. Our mixed stock and our insularity are the two formative factors in our history, from which much of our story may be seen to flow. All the great nations of Europe are mixed in their origins, and to that they largely owe the fertility and the variety of their culture. But the English nation is the product of a greater degree of mixture than most, the result of a fusion of stocks, to which two main streams have contributed in something like equal shares. In this lies perhaps a certain peculiarity, a distinctiveness at the very core of the people.

It may be that we owe to that certain characteristics which have always struck foreigners, but which are not very clear to Englishmen themselves. An impreciseness which characterizes the English mind, an absence of outline, a subtle variousness, which have made acute observers think of the people in terms of the climate. (And indeed that is another, hardly less important factor.) On one side there is the lack of clear-cutness which makes us as a people difficult for others, even for ourselves, to understand; on the other, there is a degree of instinctive sympathy, of general kindliness and tolerance, while no one can ignore the immense cultural fertility and creativeness of the people in modern history. Perhaps these characteristics, and the variety of our achievement as a nation, are due to something deep down in our very origin, the fusion of stocks from which we spring.

I have called these main streams Teuton and Celtic. By 'Teuton' I mean the peoples who came to us from around the shores of the North Sea—Angles, Saxons, Danes, Norse. Under 'Celtic' I include not only the Celts who came to us mainly from across the Channel, but also the peoples of Mediterranean stock, the Iberians as we call them, who were here before the Celts came, upon whom the Celts imposed their language and institutions, but into whom the Celts in time were racially absorbed. Nineteenth-century historians were apt to regard us simply as an Anglo-Saxon folk; in fact we are really an Anglo-Celtic people. The racial constitution of our people, with which language has nothing to do, is a great deal nearer to that of France, though the proportions are differently mixed, than it is to that of Germany.

The facts of geographical position, of our climate, the natural endowments of the soil, are no less important. They imposed their exigencies upon the men who came into the islands, until with the growth of civilization men imposed their patterns upon them. Throughout prehistory and a long way into the historic period, until in fact the Norman Conquest and the making of a strong centralized state, our insularity was no bar to invasion. The position of the islands invited invaders. But the sea-barrier and the difficulties of sea transport meant that they came over in small numbers. And that tended 'to give a unique character to the ultimate expression of any culture derived from the continent in Britain. . . Her culture at any given period represents the mingling of a number of variant elements, rather than the extension beyond the sea of a stable, definite, continental complex. . . In general, the effect of the vulnerability of Britain to invasion is that she has always tended to present successive strata of culture, and a very mixed population, the latest arrivals being dominant, and the novel culture more strongly marked in the eastern half of the island than in the western.' It may be seen that our *difference* goes back a very long way.

The first great culture which has left abiding monuments in the island and enters as a continuing factor in our stock is the megalithic culture which reached us from the Mediterranean by the Atlantic coast of Portugal, Spain, France. This was based upon the western sea-ways and spread up the Irish Sea and along the west coast of Britain to the Orkneys and Scandinavia: an astonishing achievement over centuries (2500 to 2000 B.C.) of those early sea navigators. They have left their memorials in barrows and longstones all along our western coasts, and perhaps in some of the dark population which is dominant over the western half of the island and in Ireland. Later invaders, beginning from c. 2000 B.C. with the beaker folk, have come into the island mainly from the east and south. Such were the Celtic invasions, of which the last, that of the Belgae, took place in the centuries before the Romans came; the Anglo-Saxon invasions, most important for the constitution of our people; and subsequently Danes, and Normans.

Throughout all these centuries and incursions of people by driblets, the personality of Britain itself imposed its pattern. The island is divided into two distinct zones, which afford a contrast in geography and climate: the Highland and Lowland zones. If you take a map and draw a line from Exeter in the southwest in an arc through the Severn valley to the Pennines and thence to the Tyne, you will notice that most of the Lowlands lie to the south and east, the Highlands to the north and west. In early times, invaders from the east found themselves halted or held up by the difficult Highland barrier. The Roman occupation itself epitomized the contrast between these zones in the boundary between the civil and military areas of the island. Effective Romanization was confined to the Lowlands; and the Roman failure to extend their power beyond the Forth-Clyde line strikingly illustrates the pattern which all early invasions followed.

The key to our early history then is to be found in the fact that the most habitable and conquerable areas were precisely those nearest to the invaders, whose invasions therefore cut off the west and the north from contacts with Europe. (It is like the story of Ireland, with the island of Britain playing the part of a Highland barrier.) In the Lowlands new cultures were imposed; in the Highlands they were absorbed by the older. The Highland zone tended to oust or else transform intruding elements. There was naturally far greater continuity and conservatism in the west. This pattern can be seen recurring right into our medieval and modern history, with the civil wars of the fifteenth and seventeenth centuries, its partial reversal with the Industrial Revolution. A great deal of our history, and not a little of its vigor and variety, may be due to the reactions and repercussions of the one zone upon the other, and to the underlying effort towards fusion of which we are hardly conscious as a people, but to which we may owe something of the political energy and the instinct towards expansion which have left their mark upon the world.

Britain first emerges into the light of history and becomes part of the civilized world with the Roman occupation. For some four centuries it was part of the Roman Empire: an outlying, frontier province, never an intimate part of the Empire like Southern France or Spain where the conditions of Roman life could be exactly reproduced and the population permanently Latinized. Yet it stands to reason that so long an occupation should have left enduring memorials of itself and some continuing influences. It throws a revealing light upon the character of the occupation that its chief memorial—and among the most impressive Roman monuments in any country —is Hadrian's Wall. (There is something exciting too in descending some feet below the Strand in London to come upon a Roman bath.) The chief bond which links the Britain of the Roman Empire with the Britain of today is the Christianity which the Celtic population retained in unbroken tradition.

The conquest of Britain was regarded by the Roman world, and by Caesar himself, as the logical conclusion to his conquest of Gaul. Southern Britain and Northern Gaul were intimately connected by ties of kinship, political organization, trade. The Belgic tribes in Britain sent help to the Gauls in their resistance to Caesar. The carrying trade at the western end of the Channel, which conveyed Cornish tin to the continent, was in the hands of the Veneti, the seafaring inhabitants of what is now Brittany. Everything pointed to the necessity of reducing the island. As soon as the conquest of Gaul was completed, Caesar made a reconnaissance raid across the Channel, in 55 B.C. Next year he invaded, penetrated to the center of Belgic power beyond the Thames, and reduced its head Cassivellaunus to Roman allegiance. Caesar's death postponed the conquest of Britain for some decades. Meanwhile the Belgic hegemony was continued in the long and prosperous reign, semi-civilized and Romanizing in tendency, of Cunobelinus (Shakespeare's Cymbeline), A.D. *c.* 10 - *c.* 43.

A century after Caesar, under Claudius, the conquest was taken up again in earnest, A.D. 43. In spite of the heroic resistance of Caratacus (Caradoc), the Romans in a short space of years overran the whole Lowland zone. Their difficulties began when they reached the Highland. Even so, some thirty-five years after their landing they were in effective military occupation of Wales, a feat which the Saxons failed to accomplish and the Normans achieved only after centuries. The key to the Roman success was their astonishing system of radial roads, planted with forts garrisoned by regular troops. These roads converged upon London, which became the supply base and the most important commercial center in the island. Two further legacies of the Romans to modern Britain: for London, though it shrank and declined during the dark period of the Saxon invasions, has never had a rival as a trading center since; while sections of Roman road, going straight up hill and down dale, here and there remain a feature of the landscape still.

The high-tide of Roman expansion in Britain is marked by the career of the great Agricola as governor (78 to 84). Completing the subjugation or reconquest of North Wales, Anglesey, and the north country, from the year 80 he pushed forward to the conquest of Scotland. He subdued the country up to the Forth-Clyde line and then, in co-operation with the fleet on his right flank, penetrated into Caledonia. At the battle of Mons Graupius (83) he overthrew the Caledonian power; the completion of his task was within his grasp. At that moment, by a change of policy at Rome, he was recalled. There is no doubt that Agricola planned to bring the whole island under the power of Rome and that he would have achieved it. He projected the conquest of Ireland. His recall left the task forever unfinished. The opportunity never came again. The policy of Trajan and Hadrian here was to stabilize the frontier, a policy symbolized by the erection of Hadrian's Wall from the Solway to the Tyne (123).

The Wall was a military frontier; but its building did not prevent restlessness on the part of the tribes both in front of it and in the rear. Antoninus (140) tried to subdue the Scots and got as far as building an earth and stone rampart from the Forth to the Clyde. Both this and the Wall were subsequently overrun by the vigorous tribesmen (180). Severus repaired and strengthened the Wall (205-8); and after that Rome concentrated her strength upon holding a diminished but submissive territory. Roman Britain covered roughly the modern England and Wales. There was unbroken peace for a hundred years.

Meanwhile the main lines of Roman administration had

taken shape behind the frontier. Severus divided Britain into two provinces, corresponding to the two geographical and political zones: Upper Britain, military in character, with its capital at York, Lower Britain with the seat of civil government at London. The Empire rested upon the civic foundation of Mediterranean urban life; and from the beginning a start was made to transplant these conditions with the founding of towns. There was plenty of room for self-government within the framework of the Empire, and five leading towns had the rank, and privileges, of 'colonies' conferred upon them: Verulamium (St. Albans), Colchester, Lincoln, Gloucester, York. In addition there were the tribal capitals: such places as Canterbury, Winchester, Dorchester, Exeter, Leicester. Some few have disappeared, like Caistor or Silchester; but many more have survived. And that leads us to yet another legacy of the Romans to modern Britain: the siting of many of our towns. In spite of the decay and desertion of towns during the confusion of the Saxon invasions, it is not possible to believe that there was a complete break of continuity between the Roman period and the subsequent England. The towns do not seem to have perished by fire; but there is every evidence that they shrank and decayed into neglect, their trade dried up, families of Britons living in their huts among the moldering monuments of departed Rome.

The process of decay had already started by the third century. There was a decay of city life all over Europe. The attempt to impose a Mediterranean urban civilization was failing. Roman Britain was not very prosperous economically; it was not a rich province. Tin, lead, some pearls, skins, slaves, grain were its chief commodities for export. The introduction of Roman wares, such as Samian pottery, ousted and finally quenched the output of earlier Celtic art with its more imaginative patterns, its 'dream-like quality.' Now, with the contraction of town life, the economic emphasis shifted over

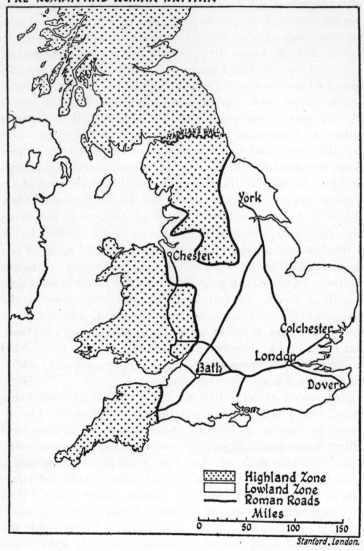

PRE-ROMAN AND ROMAN BRITAIN

HADRIAN'S WALL

York

Chester

Colchester

London

Bath

Dover

Highland Zone
Lowland Zone
Roman Roads
Miles

0   50   100   150

Stanford, London.

to the country with its flocks and herds, the life organized around the villas among the clearings, such as Chedworth in the Cotswolds. For one must not think of Roman Britain as a populous country, or see the landscape in terms of the modern countryside. It was mostly empty of people, covered with forest or moor or marsh, amid which the towns and cultivated areas, the villas, made small clearings. It must have been more like the early Frontier period in North America; and the great epic of American history, the frontier moving ever westward, has some analogy with the unrecorded history of the American pioneers' ancestors in this island a thousand years ago and more.

'The shift of population from the primary areas to the secondary has been, perhaps, the greatest change that Britain has undergone since first it began to be inhabited.' It is the essence of that economic revolution which substituted the dominance of man for the dominance of the environment. Starting with the Belgic invasions, continuing through the Roman period, it was checked for a while during the Saxon conquest. Then the Saxons took up the role with even greater energy and power; for with their heavier plows they were able to tackle the heavier soils. Following the river systems of the country they were the first people to bring order at all widely into the marshes and valley floors and turn them into English meadows, while they redoubled the attack on the forest.

But this is to anticipate. It was in the towns, and these were mainly in the south and east, that Romanization went furthest. Under the protection of Rome, the *pax Romana,* the more civilized Britons lost their vigor and independence; they became provincials, unaccustomed to the arts and ardors of war. The legions, based upon their great fortresses of York, Chester, Caerleon—a regular army of 40,000, about a tenth of the armed forces of the Empire—sheltered them from the turbulent Scots of Ireland, the Picts of Scotland. It was in the west that the vigorous tribal life of the Celts continued, and it was through them indirectly that something of Rome was transmitted to us. Above all, Christianity.

Celtic religion was very various and had no one dominant, unifying God: in that a profound reflection of the disunity which was, and always has been, the bane of the Celts. Christianity reached Britain at a very early date, and made such progress that by the third century it had reached remotest parts of the country. At the council of Arles in 314 three British bishops were present, including those of York and London.

It was in the circumstances of the disruption of the Empire that the Celts of the west displayed their greatest vigor and left enduring marks upon history. The whole barbarian world outside the frontiers was in upheaval and on the move. The weakness of the Empire at the center, an economic collapse within, invited the barbarians to attack. The process had been in being for some time; nor was it ultimately to be regretted: it meant a re-invigoration of European stocks. Historians have been all too apt to regard the end of the Roman Empire as a mysterious calamity, of which there have been endless explanations. It was perfectly natural that it should come to an end: what was extraordinary, and an astounding achievement, was that it should have lasted so long. Out of the confusion, and the re-invigoration of stocks, there came the modern nations of Europe with all their immense and varied creative fertility.

During the fourth century the Saxons across the North Sea pushed ever nearer against the frontiers. As they came in contact with Rome, so they became more affected by its influence. They took to raiding along the eastern coasts and in the Channel. Rome was forced to organize a fleet based upon a chain of forts along the southeastern coast—the Saxon Shore.

By the end of the fourth century there were gathering raids on all sides, while the legions were withdrawn to defend Rome itself. Fruitless appeals were made from Britain, the last of them as late as 446. The Irish descended upon the western coasts; the Picts of Scotland raided in the north; the Wall was swamped; the Saxons were in the Channel. The Britons were left to themselves.

It was then, in these circumstances of danger, that the western Britons experienced a revival and came into their own. It has perhaps been usual to exaggerate the disorganization and disorder of this period, to speak of 'slaughter' and 'ravages' when we should speak of incursion and colonization. After all, the country was a large one, and very empty; there was room for both Celts and Saxons. There is evidence of much going to and fro between British Christians and the continent in these years, and it is the first great missionary period of Celtic Christianity. Ninian, a Briton who had been educated at Rome, returned (c. 400) to convert the Picts to Christianity and missionize the north along the Wall. In the person of Pelagius, Britain contributed a distinguished, and perhaps a characteristic, heresy to the West: as against Augustine, Pelagius preached the freedom of the will, an emphasis to which Britons in later centuries have been prone. In St. Patrick, missionary to Ireland (432), Britain contributed a figure of European importance. St. Illtyd, another disciple of St. Germanus (who conducted missions to Britain in 429 and c. 447), was the founder of Welsh monasticism and so of a school of missionaries who have left memorials of their activities in Devon, Cornwall, and Brittany.

The fifth century saw a powerful movement of migration from western Britain to what is now Brittany. Contrary to popular belief, it was not due to Saxon or Irish pressure, but rather so much evidence of western vigor and movement at this time. Less obvious, but no less eloquent, evidence of the

reawakening of impulse is the revival of Celtic art at the end
of the Roman period, with its free and imaginative patterns
and lines. Later still, there is the curious and paradoxical fact
that out of the long period of contact and struggle between
Britons and Saxons, it was the hero of the losing side, King
Arthur, who imposed himself upon the imagination: the chief
and most lasting contribution of the Celts to the mind and
literature of Europe.

For all that, the settlement of the Northern peoples in
Britain is the governing event, or series of events, in our history. It may be regarded as forming two chapters, two periods
of immigration from across the North Sea: the first, from
c. 450 to c. 550, when the newcomers were mainly Angles and
Saxons from the northwest coast of Germany; the second,
from c. 800 to 1000, when the new arrivals upon our eastern
and northwestern shores came from Denmark and Norway.
It is a misconception to regard these two branches of the
Northern folk too closely in terms of Germany, and particularly to see them through the eyes of Tacitus, whose *Germania*
described the inland Germans whom the Romans were in
touch with on the Rhine and, even so, many centuries before
the Saxon conquest of Britain.

The essential thing about these Northern peoples is that
they were seafaring, the Norsemen even more than the English. From that simple fact we can infer how much of our
character as a people we owe to them. These Northerners had
much in common. Their languages were akin; they worshipped
the same gods, Thor and Woden; their art and their poetry
were very much alike; the heroes of their epics expressed the
same standards of conduct, mirrors in which we may still see
reflected the very soul of these Northern seafarers. In *Beowulf,*
the English epic whose hero performs his deeds in Denmark
and Scandinavia, these men 'set before themselves a high

standard of character, of loyalty to the dead no less than to the living, of discretion, of calmness in adversity, and above all, of constant valour.'

There was a strong contrast between the Britons and the Saxons. Where the former were imaginative and extreme, moody and discordant, prone to excessive asceticism or to self-indulgence, egotistical and irrational, a feminine people, the Saxons were earthy, laborious, stolid, with a greater capacity for co-operation, sticking to a job. Their greatest job was the colonization of the waste spaces of Britain. They were a virile, masculine stock: a stronger strain, when all is said, than the Celts. What more promising for the future, in spite of early hostility, difficulties of adjustment, than the marriage of two such peoples? To this amalgam, the Danes and Norse added another element: they were more electric and vital than the Saxons, with a hard, biting quality, a passionate feeling for independence, and the greatest sea folk the world has ever seen.

In the fifth century the Angles and Saxons came over, but not in large numbers. The circumstances of a sea crossing imposed their conditions as before in the unrecorded story of our prehistory. It cannot have been, as upon land, a mass migration by tribes; they came by war bands, under the leadership of fighting chiefs, some of whom had been invited by quarreling British kings. They went on coming for a century. 'The event . . . was more a colonization than a conquest.' The Romano-Britains of the southeast put up very little resistance. It was a different matter in the west, where the Welsh held out and slowed down the pace of the advance over a century and a half. And all the time the Saxons were getting more civilized, and the Welsh more accustomed to them as neighbors.

The old-fashioned view of the extermination of the Britons, even in the east and south, has long gone by the board. And from what we know of warfare among primitive peoples, as against the mass slaughter of modern warfare, it is unlikely even that there was much killing. Defeated tribes became serfs. For the rest, there was a great deal of room in the country: a Saxon community in the valley quietly subsisted alongside a British tribe in the hills, as at Fairford and Cirencester (525-70). Indeed a striking feature of the Saxon Conquest from the beginning is the extent to which the new Saxon ruling houses mingled Celtic blood in their veins.

Kent was the first kingdom to fall into the hands of the newcomers. The Kentish settlers were drawn from various folks, and their culture was a varied product, with a British strain in it, due to the survival of numbers of natives as craftsmen and serfs on the land. The Kentish state was in touch with Romanized Britons all round, and in communication above all with Frankish and Frisian lands. It lay at the meeting-point of these peoples: hence its higher culture, which was, however, a Kentish product, developed strongly within its own area, from which it overflowed into the Isle of Wight. The Romano-British population persisted on the north side of London, in the Chiltern country and the woods of Hertfordshire and Essex. Cerdic, the founder of the Wessex dynasty, which was to gain the overlordship over the English kingdoms, had a British name: he probably had a Celtic mother. Both the northern kingdoms of Deira and Bernicia took on British names; while the British kingdom of Elmet, covering the West Riding of Yorkshire, remained an independent state into the seventh century. In the north, the Angles and Celts were brought into particularly close contact, from which Northumbria emerged as the leader with an Anglo-Celtic civilization.

The second phase of the English Conquest was reached at the end of the sixth century. The kingdom of Wessex broke the British line which had held for fifty years, and reached the Severn, splitting Wales from West Wales, the southwestern peninsula. In the north there was fiercer fighting, out of which Celtic patriotism generated the name Cymry to describe their kin of Wales and Strathclyde. But the advance of the Angles to the Mersey (550-616) broke the bridge between them and turned the scale against the Britons. From that time the future of the island lay with the English. 'But the British communities in losing their language and their institutions did not for ever lose their souls; in so far as British blood continued to flow in the inhabitants of Britain, the spirit of the older race, though recessive, was not extinguished for ever.' The most permanently successful of the Saxon states, Wessex, which rose to leadership, was precisely that which had the largest admixture of Celtic population and where the fusion of peoples was most fruitful.

All the same the colonizing energy of the English altered the racial stock in this island far more than any other Teutonic invasion in other countries. In Italy, Spain, even in France, the Teutons were ultimately absorbed by the Latin population. Here there was a fusion of two peoples, a more subtle and intricate affair, which may account for much of what we are. Further, the very conditions in which the English Conquest came about may have had a profound and permanent effect upon the character of our society. An overseas migration is far more disturbing to the structure of a society than a land migration, by which a people carries its social institutions over intact into the new area. Throughout the English invasions and conquests the key figures were the chiefs, leaders of their war bands, later the kings of their folk. Their war bands became a new aristocracy. In such conditions the race was to the swiftest, power to the strongest. Individualism seems to be a fundamental characteristic of the English people; and flexibility of social structure, an absence of caste system, with a greater degree of movement within it, seems to characterize English history all through. For a time it was held up by the Norman Conquest, to re-emerge with the end of the Norman domination, such was its latent force among the English. May it not have been due to the very conditions in which they colonized this island across the North Sea, as the same flexibility of social structure and inborn sense of freedom was to be exemplified upon an even larger scale by their descendants across the oceans of the world?

The conversion of the English to Christianity was the most fruitful event in their history before the Norman Conquest. It was the result of the convergence of two streams of influence, that direct from Rome long planned by Gregory the Great who sent Augustine to England in 597, and the other coming from Iona, the missionary center of Celtic Christianity founded by Columba the Irishman, an elder contemporary of Gregory. Kent and the south received Christianity at the hands of the Roman mission, while Northumbria was converted by the Scottish missionaries, who penetrated even into Mercia and Essex. The conflict as to who was to direct English Christianity was settled in favor of Rome by the Synod of Whitby (664), and was followed up by the appointment of the Greek, Theodore of Tarsus, as Archbishop of Canterbury. 'This was the first Archbishop whom all the English Church obeyed.' He organized the church in England, giving it system and law by his synods and canons. He was 'the first statesman to appear in the story of England.'

There followed a brilliant period in early English civilization, centered mainly in Northumbria, whose culture was the product of the fusion of English and Celtic influences: a beacon-light in the north that shone out across the wastes of the Dark Ages. Its greatest figure was Bede (673-735), whose *Ecclesiastical History of the English People* has 'a place apart from all other histories written in the Dark Ages.' His was 'the first English mind which speaks to the modern world fully and lucidly on a wide range of subjects.' A personality that comes to us across the centuries radiant, human, undimmed, full of charm, and very recognizably English. The Devonshireman Boniface (675-754) has an even greater place in the history of Europe. The great missionary who brought Germany within the fold of Christianity, who organized the German church and reformed the Frankish, is a figure who affected world history. In all, this early period was 'not only the most remarkable in the history of our pre-Norman ancestors, but can claim comparison with the ages of the greatest vitality in medieval and modern England. . . The Conversion, more truly than the age of the Renaissance, gave Englishmen a new heaven and a new earth.'

This period, though its effects were lasting, was brought to an end by the Danish Invasions. A profound disturbance shook the Scandinavian world, and an expansive energy carried the Northmen across the northern seas, into the Channel and the Mediterranean. In the ninth century, Britain was constantly raided by the long swift Danish warships, superior in craftsmanship and in their handling to Saxon skill. Soon they were followed by regular campaigning armies, which ravaged and wintered in the land. The country was thrown into confusion, and much of the ground the English had gained culturally was lost. Out of the mêlée one heroic figure emerges, Alfred king of Wessex (850-99), who saved Wessex from the Danes and prevented them from conquering the island. After indescribable efforts and with the greatest courage and tenacity, he succeeded in beating the Northmen and forcing a peace upon them by which he divided the country with them, the boundary running across the midlands along the Roman Watling Street. To the east lay the areas of Danish settlement: the Danelaw, mainly Yorkshire, Lincoln, and East Anglia.

Alfred is one of the great figures of history because his career ensured the future of England to the English stock. After his hard-won victories he reorganized the West Saxon state, built a fleet, and so became the founder of English maritime power. He then set to work to repair the cultural ravages of war; he called in the Welsh bishop, Asser, to aid him in educating himself and his people, translating books into English and becoming the founder of English prose literature. There is something infinitely appealing and simple in the personality of this man which reaches out to us across a thousand years; as with Bede, 'we feel him to be unlike the men of other nations, but like the best among ourselves.'

Alfred's successors brought the Danelaw into submission and achieved a formal unity of the nation under the headship of Wessex. But their work was undone by the second wave of Danish invasions, which attacked southern England from c. 1000. This time there was no Alfred to oppose them. Attempts were made to buy off the Danes with Danegeld, a tax which drained the wealth of the country, and was of the first importance in its effects upon social, economic, and administrative life. The country submitted to the rule of the great Canute, who brought England into the orbit of his Scandinavian Empire (1016-36). His policy was to reconcile English and Danes upon a basis of equality and acceptance of Christianity.

The Danes were vigorous traders, who revived the life of the Roman towns in the north and greatly increased the commerce of London. They were freer and more independent than the Saxons; the Danelaw contained many freemen, but no slaves, in contrast to the south and west. They contributed a most valuable element to the mixture of stocks in Britain, mingling easily with the English and concentrating chiefly in Yorkshire, Lincoln, East Anglia, and the Lake District. But Canute's Empire broke up with his death: the future of England was not to be with Scandinavia.

The strongest and most highly organized state in Europe was that which the Northmen had built up across the Channel—Normandy. The Normans combined all the energy and vigor of their Viking ancestors with Latin culture, the highest in Europe. The end of Canute's empire disclosed the weakness of the English state left to its own resources, with the centrifugal tendencies represented in the ancient kingdoms. The English had not fulfilled their earlier promise. There was something easy-going, kindly, slack about them. They would need a harder school of discipline, a stronger impact still, before they achieved unity as a nation. That impact, a catastrophe for the English at the time, but ultimately far-reaching and beneficent in its effects, was to come from Normandy. England was to be laid open by force to the embrace of the continent at its most powerful and highly organized point.

II. Medieval England

THE Norman Conquest of England is a fact of prime importance in our history and a decisive event in European history. Hitherto, England had lain with Scandinavia on the outermost fringe of civilization, loosely connected with the continent. Henceforth she was to be closely bound up with France. The medieval period may be defined as that in which influences coming from France were dominant. The character of the Middle Ages is given by the fact that the center of gravity of civilization had shifted away from the Mediterranean, northwards to France and the Rhine. Britain was still an outpost, but much nearer the creative center of medieval civilization; its cultural contacts were close and intimate now as compared with earlier centuries. During the whole medieval period this country followed a parallel development to France, with similar institutions political and social, and a predominantly French culture. It was only towards the end of the Middle Ages that England came to find herself.

During the long reign of Edward the Confessor, the last king of the line of Alfred, Norman influences came seeping into the country. Edward himself was wholly Norman in his sympathies, appointed Normans to bishoprics, surrounded himself with Norman influences. Norman traders were given privileges in the country, a Norman earldom constituted on the Welsh border, and the abbey of Westminster, in which Edward wished to leave his personal imprint rather than in offspring, was built in the new Romanesque style. His fixing the royal palace at Westminster, hard by the abbey, outside of London, had an important influence: it left London free to play an immense part in the winning of English liberties in the future.

Edward's death left a disputed succession. The country was invaded simultaneously by a Norse claimant in the north, and by William of Normandy, claiming the succession to his cousin, in the south. Harold defeated the Northern invader and returned to meet William at Hastings. The battle was a trial between the old Nordic method of warfare against the new continental methods: footmen fighting with battle-axes against horsemen wielding spear and sword and supported by archers. William was completely victorious, was accepted by the Witan as king and crowned at Westminster; but the country continued its sullen resistance.

Above all in the north. The Anglo-Danes there had held aloof from the struggle in the south. They were to receive a terrible lesson. William carried out a systematic devastation of Northumbria from York to Durham, combined with a good deal of harrying of the Midlands as he came and went. After that there was no further possibility of resistance or effective rebellion. In time Durham Castle and the Cathedral rose above the scene of devastation: a splendid symbol of the new, ruthless, and logical Latin civilization. Norman feudalism was imposed upon the freer foundations of northern society, as well as upon the south and west.

The Conquest was a very terrible experience for the English. The invasion had been organized as a joint-stock enterprise for sharing out the rich, inviting lands of Britain. There were not more than 5000 knights, among them Bretons and Flemings as well as Frenchmen, to be enfeoffed by the Conqueror. That small number with their armed retainers held down a population of a million and a half: evidence of the backwardness of old English society compared with the continent. Immediately after Hastings the confiscation of Saxon estates began, and it went on gradually all over the country until the Saxon landowning class was completely displaced by the Norman barons. They formed a new governing class clamped down upon the backs of the English: a hard and ruthless military caste, with a code of their own, with their own idea of law, and everywhere their stone castles going up all over the land as symbols of their domination, their watchfulness, amid an alien people. The English were outlawed from power. For three centuries they were a submerged people.

The process was not inevitable; it need not have been so savage; it could have been carried through with more justice. Yet who can say that it was not in its ultimate effects beneficial?

To take one very striking point. In all the centuries before the Norman Conquest, Britain had been again and again subjugated. After the Conquest, never. For the Normans had transplanted a strong, centralized state to this island. Moreover, it is obvious that the country needed licking into shape, and that only an iron hand could forge a unified nation out of the many elements that had poured into the island. In fact, it is also clear that by the end of the Saxon period only an alien governing military caste could do it. It lay in the logic of history that the Normans should provide that caste: theirs was the most highly organized state of the day, just across the Channel. They brought with them their own peculiar institutions which showed themselves capable of an immense and flexible development when transplanted into new territory. But it was our good fortune that the Conquest gave us a long line of most vigorous and statesmanlike kings.

The Conqueror showed that great qualities of statesmanship went along with his ruthlessness. Reconstruction of the institutions of the state went hand in hand with the reform of the church. The candidate of the Papacy, he brought the new inspiration of the Cluniac reforms into England. The Anglo-Saxon church, in spite of the reforming effort of Dunstan, was corrupt, decadent, secular. The courts dealt with a mingle-mangle of secular and spiritual affairs; the Witan concerned itself with ecclesiastical as well as political matters; it was all very Erastian, very English. William sorted this out. He divided the church courts from the secular courts: a reform which prepared the way for the conflict between the spheres of church and state all through the Middle Ages. With such men as Lanfranc and Anselm beside the Norman kings, the best spirit of Rome returned to England. The movement was pressed forward for a purer and stricter monastic life, a higher standard of learning and morals among the clergy; way was made for the reception of Canon Law. At the same time William and his successors were determined that within their dominions the church should be subordinate to the state.

Their kingship was the strongest in Europe. By the very fact of conquest all powers proceeded from the king. When parceling out lands to his followers William saw to it that the Crown was the strongest holder in every county; and he exacted allegiance from tenants to himself before any other lord. The introduction of military tenures on the land and the creation of a feudal army were revolutionary changes of the first importance. Feudalism was indeed characteristic of the European society of the time: it meant the organization of social and governmental structure in all its aspects, military, economic, political, judicial, on a local basis. It made for stability in society, after the confusion and disturbance of the great era of migrations. It was the foundation of the stability of the Middle Ages. The aim of the great medieval minds was to provide men with such a permanent resting-place, a fabric to inhabit: the stable structure on earth mirrored in the ordered hierarchy of heaven depicted on the walls of their churches.

England became a feudal society, as Europe was feudal. The

Conquest gave it that stable foundation and framework. Where Anglo-Saxon tenure had been much slacker, dependent on the shifts and changes of personal ties, Norman tenure was coherent, logical, permanent. The danger of feudalism was the excessive power of local territorial magnates with their powers of private jurisdiction. The Norman kings used their rights as successors to the English kings to ward against this. In Anglo-Saxon England there were the shire courts and the hundred courts under royal control. With the Conquest manorial courts sprang up all over the land. But the kings were careful to keep control of the sheriffs in the counties as royal officers and to see that the post did not become hereditary. Out of the marriage of old Saxon institutions and laws with Norman, the laws and liberties of England were evolved.

From very early on, the kings used the native English as a counterpoise to the power of the baronage; so that England saw a controlled feudalism at work, not an uncontrolled such as rendered the contemporary kings of France less powerful than their vassals. The Conqueror himself led a force of Englishmen combined with Normans for service overseas against Le Mans. The English came to look increasingly to the kingship as the expression of national as against baronial interests. The Conqueror's son, Henry I, married an Englishwoman, descendant of the old royal line—to the merriment of the barons. But his hand was as strong upon them as his father's had been; and his introduction of scutage, a money payment in place of military service, first controlled and then eventually displaced the Conqueror's armed host.

The Norman genius for order and detail in administration, where the Anglo-Saxons were more lax and easy-going, is witnessed by its most famous monument, Domesday Book. A distinguished Russian historian, Dr. Savine, has told us that the history of English administration is no less remarkable than our so much better-known constitutional history. Domesday Book is its first and most remarkable record, from which so many others and so unbroken an administrative tradition have followed. It was a fiscal survey of the whole country, of men, their holdings of land and animals, the whole thing classified from the point of view of their wealth and taxable capacity: a kind of census of the resources of the country, which 'if due regard be paid to the conditions of its execution may claim to rank as the greatest record of medieval Europe.' The Anglo-Saxon chronicler was ashamed of such prying scrutiny into private affairs: 'So minutely did he cause it to be investigated that there was not one hide or yard of land, nor even (it is shameful to write of it, though he thought it not shameful to do it) an ox nor a cow nor a swine that was not set down in his writ. And all the writings were brought to him afterwards.' It is a very English reaction, recognizable across the ages.

These gains survived the baronial anarchy of Stephen's reign. Henry II, one of the greatest men in medieval history, a ruler with an essentially legal turn of mind, was responsible for the next phase of national development. The head of a great empire extending from the Pyrenees to Scotland, he was well able to control his baronage and proceed with his work of building a state. He extended the authority of the king's courts over all the land, against the private jurisdictions of the barons. He introduced the jury system, in place of primitive modes of ordeal, compurgation, or trial by battle: a system which had a great development before it and which became the pride of the English before the Middle Ages were over. Out of Henry's work there developed the 'Common Law,' in place of the variegated provincial customs of earlier times.

The 'Common Law'—a key to much in our subsequent history—means the traditional law common to the whole land; as distinguished from statutes and ordinances, or from local customs, or from ecclesiastical law, which was ruled by the principles of Roman Law. The Common Law was temporal and customary, gradually built up, like a coral reef, from innumerable concrete cases and decisions. Thus it had an innate capacity for adapting itself to varied social circumstances and needs, while it answered to something deep in the English nature that does not like to commit itself to large general propositions and the tyranny of the abstract. Hence its immense future with the English-speaking peoples: something which marks us off from the continent brought up under the aegis of Roman Law. This development from early on had the effect of making law itself the arbiter, rather than the will of the prince; and so it has played a political role of the first importance in our history, reinforcing the secular movement towards freedom.

Only the church administered a check to Henry, who sought to control its immunity from lay jurisdiction and bring it within the framework of the royal courts. St. Thomas Becket won in his duel with the King by his martyrdom at Canterbury, the effect of which was to bring England into line with the rest of Europe. For three hundred years the church retained its immunity until a later Henry, Henry VIII, destroyed it with a greater logical completeness than in any other country, and turned the church in England into the servant of the state. Actually the twelfth century was a period of immense progress and expansion for the church. All over the country there was a fever of church-building; scores of monasteries were founded; the Cistercian movement reached the country, gave a great impulse to monasticism and, not less important, played a pioneer part in bringing the waste spaces of the north back into cultivation. Perhaps the most fundamental achievement of the age, a silent process that was underlying all that was spectacular and brilliant on the surface, was the vast internal colonization of the land, the spread of cultivation going on all the time.

Internal peace was converting the feudal baronage into country gentlemen. Their solid tangible estates, and the increase of their yield, were what most mattered to them: their real life, as against the intricate formulae of feudal history. There was very little of a bureaucratic tradition in medieval England: the Crown depended largely upon the amateur services of the local gentry; on their side there grew up a deep, an instinctive tradition of service, an innate sense of responsibility, to which England has owed much in her history. It goes right back to the early Middle Ages, and is a leading theme in our story, though one that English people take so much for granted, they are hardly conscious of its importance.

The institution of primogeniture meant that a whole class of younger sons were left to make their own way, by adventure, or going into commerce or the church. Its effect was therefore towards a freer society than on the continent, where the social structure had greater class-rigidity. Birth in England was never all in all; a man could make his way by his talents, and English history is full, from the great Hubert Walter or Stephen Langton onwards, of statesmen and ecclesiastics who owed nothing of their influence to their birth, and everything to their abilities. There was no rigid exclusion of commerce. From early on, money made in trade began to marry land. All this increased social flexibility. At the same time it strengthened the unity of society: the lesser gentry were in touch with the burghers of the towns, most of all in London, the position of which in the country's trade was vastly greater in medieval times than today, and which was no less a microcosm of the country's life. The alliance between the gentry on the land and the middle classes of the towns becomes the backbone of our constitutional history: in time it governed the country. Perhaps that may account for the fact that English medieval towns were not revolutionary, in contrast to the continental communes. When trouble came, it came mostly from the baronage, or at times from a revolt of the peasantry.

The baronage itself was not exclusive; it contained within its ranks men of very varied holdings, and it was ready to ally itself with other classes when it was necessary to restrain a tyrannical or correct an incompetent king. This was the meaning of the movement it headed against John, and the reason for its success. John had lost the continental heritage of Henry II, including even Normandy, had quareled with the church and brought an interdict down upon the country, and alienated large sections of his people. The strength of the baronage against John was that it did express the demands of the classes which had drawn together, and in that sense Magna Carta which it forced him to grant was a national charter. It was in fact only a statement of the demands of those classes for *their* 'liberties'; though the very demand opened the way for wider liberties later. This was the way through to the future. The posthumous history of the Charter was to have an extraordinary importance in the story of English liberty.

The next step in broadening the basis of government, ultimately the most important of all for the extension of liberties, was to call representatives of the people into consultation—in a word, into Parliament. It so happens that this step was taken (1265) by the pure Frenchman, Simon de Montfort, who was the leader of the English people against Henry III, became their first great hero and martyr to their cause. His precedent was followed by Henry's son, the great Edward I, with whom the work of the Norman kings in state-building reached its apogee. The English state, centralized, efficient, powerful, was complete, with its institutions in shape and functioning.

There is nothing peculiar to England in the institution of Parliament. About this time Parliaments were summoned in most states of western Europe from Spain to Hungary. What was peculiar to England was the successful development of parliamentary government. This was the result of centuries, and of conditions peculiar to England. In the first place, it was due to the very strength of the monarchy. In other countries the great feudatories or the communes were so powerful that they fought for their own independence. That was impossible in England; the state the Norman kings had made was too strong. In consequence the struggle of classes for power had to take place within this framework; the movement for freedom expressed itself at the center, instead of spending itself in the struggle for local independence. And with most beneficial results in establishing liberties co-operatively. It may be that we owe to this a fundamental characteristic at the root of English history, that the struggle of classes for power has usually been contained within the framework of the state without breaking it. Then too the country was small enough for effective centralized government. France, Spain, Germany, Italy were too large in the feudal circumstances of the Middle Ages and with its primitive communications.

Edward I frequently called national assemblies, or Parliaments, into consultation and this must have made for the political education of the country. His reign saw the beginning of our statute law; his land legislation in and through Parliament became the starting-point of our modern land law. It had the effect of multiplying the number of tenants-in-chief of the Crown and so leveling down the great feudal baronies: the beginning of the long career and the success of the gentry in our history. In Parliament the gentry sat with the representatives of the towns in the Commons; the great barons sat apart. So that Parliament was not divided according to estates as elsewhere in Europe. Since the Commons were so widely representative of the country, they became increasingly consulted in matters of taxation; and that accounts for a great extension of their power in the later Middle Ages.

With so strongly developed a state, it was natural that England, from being the recipient of foreign influences, should begin to give out of her own, pass from the defensive to the active and aggressive. With their immense continental lands and responsibilities it was not worth while for the early medieval kings to embark on the conquest of Ireland, Scotland, Wales: they were too poor to attract. Henry II left Strongbow to plant Anglo-Norman dominion in Ireland, but the subjugation of the country was never properly taken in hand during the Middle Ages. Wales experienced a national revival under Llewelyn the Great, who reunited the country. In a series of campaigns Edward I subjugated it, organized the Principality into shires, constituted it an appanage of his eldest son, the first 'Prince of Wales,' and left memorials of himself in the chain of great castles, like Conway and Caernarvon. Later, in the fifteenth century, there was another revival of Welsh nationalism under Owen Glendower (1400-1415). Indeed, the Welsh people never became reconciled to English rule until they gave a dynasty to the English Crown, the Tudors, the greatest of our royal lines.

Edward I was well on the way to a similar reduction of Scotland when he died. His incompetent successor Edward II lost the fruits of his father's efforts at Bannockburn, one of the decisive battles of the Middle Ages, for it determined the independence of Scotland for the next three hundred years. Scotland remained independent, but poor, uncivilized, on the northern fringe.

The real force of the strong, united English state was exerted against France. It led to the Hundred Years' War, with all its age-long consequences for both countries. Its origin was to be found in the determination of the English kings to hold on to, or even recover, something of their inheritance

in France, and in the equal determination of the French kings
to drive them or keep them out. Beneath this there was the
natural attraction of a much richer, more highly civilized land,
at the same time less well organized and divided within itself, for a strong, well-knit state like England with its fighting
aristocracy. It was just like the attraction Italy had for the
medieval Germans, and for the Renaissance French.

The Hundred Years' War fell into two parts. The first covered roughly the reign of Edward III and the career of his
famous son, the Black Prince, pattern of the European chivalry of the time. There was peace, with a great deal of restless
activity at home during the reigns of Richard II and Henry
IV. Then the second wave of aggression was started by the
young conqueror Henry V, and lasted for years, until it spent
itself well on in the reign of his passive, saintly son Henry VI.
It was immediately followed by the outbreak of civil war
among rival factions of the fighting nobility, the Wars of the
Roses, in which they exhausted their strength and made way
for the rise of the gentry, whose power along with the town
middle class constituted the main support of the new and most
successful dynasty, the Tudors.

The war began with the first great naval victory in our history, off Sluys on Midsummer Day 1340. Its importance was
that it secured communications with our allies, the Flemish
towns, and from that time forward the mastery of the Channel
was the chief aim of our maritime policy. The Flemish manufacturing towns were the main market for English wool, upon
which they were wholly dependent. Throughout the war with
France they were our allies, while the French-speaking aristocracy of the Low Countries were allies of feudal France.
The fact was that the French state was out of date compared
with the more compact and unified English state, resting on a
broader and more popular basis; otherwise the latter, alto-

gether smaller and poorer, would never have achieved so much success. This social difference was reflected in the character of the opposing armies. In the great pitched battles of Crecy, Poitiers, Agincourt, the English archers with their longbow—which they had adopted from the Welsh—routed the heavy French feudal cavalry with great slaughter. The combination of archers and foot soldiers, drawn from the ranks of yeomen and townsmen, was everywhere showing itself superior to the heavy, indisciplined, mailed horsemen of feudalism. The French made an effort to copy English tactics after Crecy. But to produce yeomen archers would have meant a revolutionary change in the French social structure. It was not until towards the end of the Hundred Years' War, with the rise of gunpowder and artillery, that the French were able to draw level with the English archers. Meanwhile their best reply was to follow Fabian tactics, avoiding pitched battles, and wearing the small English forces down. The latter ravaged across the rich lands of France, but at the end of the war they were left in possession only of Calais.

It was the wool trade that largely enabled the country to finance these long wars. Throughout a great part of the Middle Ages England was the largest source of fine wool in Europe, and so had a key position in the economic system which interlocked the cloth-manufacturing with the pasture-farming countries. During the two centuries after the Conquest the Low Countries were our chief market and the Flemings predominant in the English trade. But a good part of the Florentine industry was also dependent upon English wool, and the Italians succeeded to the dominant position of the Flemings.

The war with France necessitated the organization of the wool trade and the exploitation of its resources to finance the government. The foreigners were extruded by state action and an English monopoly was set up. English wool had certain superior qualities essential to fine cloth-making and the Government took advantage of this natural monopoly to levy very heavy export duties which the foreigner had to pay, in the absence of an alternative source of supply. So raw wool financed the earlier part of the Hundred Years' War. But this very process played its part in increasing the manufacture of cloth in this country. From the fifteenth century England became the leading cloth-exporting country, a great economic gain, and carried most of the export in her own ships. The wool trade was therefore a dominating concern in commerce and politics. It largely financed the war; it dictated the alliance with the Low Countries—a permanent feature in our policy; it played a considerable part in the constitutional struggles which ended with the Commons in control of taxation. And the control of taxation was the chief element in the rise of the Commons to a key position in our political system.

The wool trade was the first source of English prosperity, the first to give us a disposable surplus of wealth. It may be said to be the foundation of England's commercial greatness. Every English schoolboy knows that the seat of the Lord Chancellor in the House of Lords is a woolsack, and that is why. But there are indeed ubiquitous memorials in England of what we owe to wool in the past. In the Yorkshire dales, in the Severn and Wye valleys there are the ruins of the great Cistercian abbeys which grew the wool upon those hillsides and first made a business of it. The second phase when we took to manufacturing ourselves may be seen in the splendid parish churches of the clothing districts of East Anglia and the west country, Somerset and Devon. In that phase the small grower of wool became more characteristic, and the merchants who collected it from him have left their monuments in the great churches of the Cotswolds and the woolen towns. The rise of the middlemen merchants to a position of dominance and final control of the trade had important social consequences: it prevented the emergence of the big financier and helped to establish a large and substantial middle class. In its strength and the effect it has had in increasing social cohesion lies much of the subsequent success of our history and its difference from those countries which have had no strong middle class. It helps to account for the likeness and understanding between us and the Netherlands, Switzerland, and Scandinavia.

The later Middle Ages witnessed a profound disturbance in the social conditions and status of the people at large, especially the peasantry upon whom society rested and out of whose labor came the cathedrals, abbeys, churches, castles, the chivalry, magnificent display, the costumes, extravagance, and indeed the culture, the leisured learning of the time. Feudalism rested upon villeinage, which meant that the peasantry was for the most part tied to the soil, in bondage. Nothing is more noticeable in the early Middle Ages than the utter passivity of the mass of the people: they were beasts of burden: their silence may be heard. But in the fourteenth century they began to stir. The natural progress of society was bringing about a change from field labor services to payments of rent in money; the increasing use of money helped on the emancipation of the villeins, which was shattering the economic form of the medieval world and giving poor men personal freedom. The process was hastened, and rendered inevitable, by the Black Death which raged over Europe and fell upon England in 1348-9. At least a quarter of the population of some four millions was killed off. The market value of labor was doubled at a stroke. It was impossible for landowners to arrest the gains of the peasantry. Their attempts to do so brought about the Peasants' Revolt of 1381, a revolutionary disturbance which affected many English counties: one form of the social unrest which swept over the Continent in those years. But the emancipation of the villeins could not be held up, and indeed the process was largely completed in the fifteenth century.

Culturally too the English people were waking to life. In the early Middle Ages they received from abroad perhaps more than they gave out; in the course of the period the balance changed. Even to the twelfth-century Renaissance England had something to contribute: Geoffrey of Monmouth began a new epoch in European literature with his *History of the Kings of Britain*, which launched the Arthurian legend upon its astonishing and prolific career. John of Salisbury and Gerald of Wales were the greatest men of letters of the age. *Opus anglicanum*, needlework after the English pattern, held a place of its own: the famous Bayeux tapestry is of English, not Norman, workmanship. Gothic architecture developed simultaneously in England and France; it is not certain whether the Gothic arch was not first developed at Durham. In Henry II's reign a migration of students from Paris began the university of Oxford, from which a further migration started Cambridge. Oxford retained an undoubted supremacy all through the Middle Ages, until, with the Reformation, Cambridge drew level, and in mathematics and the sciences took the lead.

The thirteenth century witnessed the coming of the friars to England; and the school of Oxford Franciscans made a profound impression upon Europe. It produced Roger Bacon, foremost of medieval scientists, Duns Scotus and William of Ockham, among the most brilliant and original of medieval philosophers. The rapid growth of law in this period is witnessed by a great law-book, that of the jurist Bracton, the first full and comprehensive treatise on the laws of England. Though influenced by Roman principles in its attempt to order, it is very English in spirit and so much evidence that English law was already becoming 'case-law.' Nor was there wanting a great, and very English, historian in Matthew Paris.

Up to this time English culture expressed itself, like the rest of Europe, mainly in Latin. But from the fourteenth century a note of its own is heard: its own contribution to Europe. The English language reaches its spring-time maturity with the poetry of Chaucer, first of our long line of great poets. In his wonderful poem *Piers Plowman,* William Langland reached back to the old alliterative poetry of the early English and gave it final expression. Wyclif attacked the privileges of the church and anticipated the line subsequently taken by the Reformation with his lay point of view. He was the intellectual inspiration of the Lollards, a Protestant sect which was driven underground among the people but never wholly extinguished and lasted on to link up with the Reformation in England. Wyclif's doctrines had a notable influence abroad upon John Hus and so had a further link with the Reformation in central Europe. In the next century, Sir Thomas Malory produced a great prose masterpiece with his *Morte d'Arthur.* Again King Arthur, and the 'matter of Britain'!

Meanwhile, England had achieved a new architectural style of its own: Perpendicular, as opposed to French 'flamboyant.' Another sign that in the course of the Hundred Years' War, the two countries most intimately connected in Europe, so much so that they formed a joint Anglo-French civilization, were drawing apart. Much of the finest of our later medieval architecture, in cathedrals, parish churches, colleges of which the fifteenth century was prolific, in manor-houses, is in this indigenous style, restrained, noble, completely satisfying, with something classical in its perfect proportions. At the same time a school of native music was growing up which produced in John Dunstable a composer of European fame. Nor is the

music of that early time altogether dead so long as Englishmen remember the lovely song

> Sumer is icumen in

or the trumpet note of

> Our King went forth to Normandy.

Above all, the language came into its own, the speech of
the submerged English, who now absorbed their French-
speaking aristocracy, the first step upon its unimaginable
career of becoming a world language. The centuries of conquest and submergence had had a most important effect: prolonged contact, first with Danish, then with French, had
rubbed off the inflexions of old English and made the language taut, supple, simple. It was the simplicity which is 'a
product of high civilization, not a primitive condition.' Re-
maining essentially English in its bone structure, it became a
'half-sister to the Romance languages' in its vocabulary, so
large were its importations of French and Latin words. In
that, the English language faithfully reflects the tolerant,
mixed character of its stocks, the creativeness of fusion. It was
not until the fourteenth century that a 'standard' English
emerged: the speech of the East Midlands, of London and the
two universities, the language of Chaucer and of Wyclif's
translations from the Bible. Henry V was the first king to use
English in his official correspondence. By the fifteenth century
the English aristocracy was having to learn the language of
their Norman ancestors as a foreign tongue.

The second phase of the Hundred Years' War enormously
increased the sentiment of nationalism in both England and
France; the two countries which had been so closely associated
drew apart. Both countries owe it, however, to the struggle,
which was in other respects so deplorable, that they achieved
nationality earlier and more easily than most. Still nothing

can excuse Henry V's war upon France, certainly not the fact that he was called in by one party to a civil war, nor even his own Napoleonic cast of mind which urged him on to the conquest of Jerusalem. His early death, after achieving the succession to the French Crown in his astonishing brief career, put an end to all his plans. The English, with their altogether smaller resources, could not hope to hold France against the will of the French people once that was aroused. And its latent strength was aroused and brought to point in the career of Joan of Arc, who set in motion the forces which finally drove the English from France. Two years after their expulsion, civil war, the 'Wars of the Roses,' began within the ranks of the English nobility, which was to end their ascendancy and make way for a new order.

In 1399 a revolution of the upper classes, very like that of 1688, had displaced Richard II, the legitimate representative of the Plantagenet line, who aimed at making himself an absolute monarch, in favor of the head of a junior branch of the line, Henry IV. From that there sprang the faction fights between the two houses, York and Lancaster, which filled the politics of the fifteenth century with discord and provided Shakespeare with material for his historical plays. The Wars of the Roses bled the baronage white; the country was distracted by the campaigns and the excursions of the magnates of late bastard feudalism, the 'over-mighty subjects' who were an almighty nuisance and whom the average citizen would gladly see reduced to order. This beneficent work was to be achieved by a renewed strengthening of the monarchy, under the influence of Renaissance ideas of the state, and based upon the gentry and the town middle class. It was the end of medieval England.

III. The National State

THE discovery of America is the capital event in the history of the modern world and was decisive for the fortunes of this country. Before that the Mediterranean countries and the routes leading to them retained their ancient leadership. The opening-up of ocean routes across the Atlantic to a New World had the effect of shifting the emphasis of power to the western coast of Europe. Spain and Portugal profited first, but in the end the shift of power moved to the northwest, where England lay at the very nodule of the shortest crossings of the Atlantic. This development was not merely due to geographical good fortune. That state which could best adapt itself to the new conditions would out-distance rivals. It happened that England did. The work of turning the country into a modern nation-state and gaining a place in the New World was achieved by a remarkable line of rulers, the Tudors (1485-1603).

The first of them, Henry VII, was a cautious calculating Welshman who had seen much adversity in his youth. He resisted the temptation to foreign adventures, of which England had had too much, and concentrated upon reducing the power of the nobles who had made the Wars of the Roses. Abroad, he made the alliance with Spain which lasted for nearly a century, determined the lines of our foreign policy through the changes of the Reformation, and conditioned our Atlantic and oceanic enterprise up to 1569, when the alliance came to an end. At home he was bent upon building up a more efficient administrative system, bringing new and able men of the middle class into high office, relying upon

the gentry for local government of the countryside. Throughout the sixteenth century and later, the power and importance
of the gentry as justices of the peace increased: they provided
the steel framework of government in the country. They were
unofficial, in a sense amateur, unpaid. There was no standing
army; yet the country at large, except for a few crises, maintained order. It was a remarkable achievement.

Under the Tudor monarchy, the country attained a greater
degree of natural unity than ever before. Crown, gentry, middle class, people at large were in harmony; monarch and Parliament worked hand in hand. So the many dangers of this
period of growth, expansion, adventure, revolutionary change
in Europe, were triumphantly surmounted and England
launched upon her career of success as a modern power.
Henry VII and indeed most of the Tudors were in touch
with commercial interests and anxious to advance them. Both
he and his granddaughter Elizabeth, first and last of the line,
were keenly interested in voyages of discovery and oceanic
enterprise.

It is not generally realized how large a share the English
had in the discovery of America. Some years before the voyage
of Columbus, expeditions were sent out from Bristol westward into the Atlantic to search for rumored islands. Bristol
was in touch with Iceland, where the knowledge of the tenth-
century discoveries in North America, Greenland, and Mark-
land had not died out. Bristol's trade with Spain and Portugal, and later with Madeira and the Azores, linked up with
Spanish and Portuguese voyages into the Atlantic. Cabot
brought these early efforts to a point with his new Renaissance
ideas on world geography and the possibilities of the Atlantic.
He laid his plans before the success of Columbus was known,
and with the interest and encouragement of Henry VII
piloted the first English ship across to the coast of Nova Scotia
and Newfoundland in 1497. On his second voyage he disap-

peared with all hands. But it seems that the English were among the first to recognize that it was a new continent that had been discovered, and not, as Columbus insisted, the outlying coast of Asia. That realization was the effective 'discovery' of America.

After so early and so promising a start England fell back somewhat in the race, while Spain expanded her power in the Caribbean and Central America, Portugal in Africa and round the Cape to India and the Far East. The first part of Henry VIII's reign was wasted in playing an expensive, an extravagant part in European diplomacy in the rivalry between France and the Hapsburgs, under the aegis of a brilliant but essentially (if not literally) sterile Cardinal, Wolsey, whose long rule turned out to be the last throw of the medieval church in England. His downfall opened the floodgates of the Reformation.

The occasion which gave their head in this country to the new forces that were astir all over northern Europe was the question of Henry's divorce from Catherine of Aragon. It was vitally necessary that Henry should have a son to secure the succession. Of Catherine he had only a daughter, Mary— and a woman had never yet ruled in England. He was persuaded that his marriage to his brother's widow was invalid, and pressed the Pope to dissolve it. Unfortunately the Pope was under the thumb of the Emperor Charles V, who was Catherine's nephew, and so Henry could not be accommodated. The question became immensely complicated, a European *cause célèbre*. Henry was theologically orthodox and had even written a book in defense of the Catholic position against Luther, so earning him that title of 'Defender of the Faith' from the Papacy which still appears among the titles of English kings and upon our coinage. (We are a conservative people in such matters.)

Henry did not wish personally for a break with Rome; but

he was a man of immensely strong will, under the pressure of political necessity and personal passion. His decision to break away from the Roman obedience removed the chief barrier to the Reformation influences which were sweeping Germany and indeed all northern Europe. Hitherto the monarchy and the great Cardinal had stood between them and this country. Now the latent forces which had been gathering within the country over centuries against Rome came to a head. Men remembered Wyclif and the defeats which English kings, like Henry II and John, had suffered at the hand of the church. An underground tradition of Lollard sectarianism linked up with the new Protestant doctrines coming in from the Continent, especially through the eastern seaports into the most active and progressive parts of the country, London, Kent, East Anglia, Cambridge. There was a widespread and deep-rooted feeling against the privileges of the church, an ancient anti-clericalism, combined with a genuine desire, shared by the best men of all parties, Erasmus, Sir Thomas More, Cranmer, Cardinal Pole, for church reform. Among the propertied classes there was a still more ardent desire for the wealthy possessions, the lands of the church.

The strong support Henry got for his breach with Rome was an expression of all these forces and, underneath, of that rising nationalism which was the new and revolutionary movement of the age shattering the old medieval order with its universal church. England, with other northern countries, was determined to be independent of foreign dominion, to accept no tutelage, to throw off the vestiges of ancient subjection, which had yet cradled them and tutored them in their childhood. These nations were determined to assert their maturity and have their head. It is a mistake to regard a movement so fundamental, so revolutionary a development, in purely personal or even sectarian terms. There was something inevitable about it; perhaps the Reformation itself is to be regarded as part of the changed emphasis of power from the southern to the northern nations. The latter would no longer accept the old leadership of the south; Canterbury, no more than Wittenberg or Geneva, the headship of Rome.

In England the Reformation impulses were controlled and directed by the state at every point; in consequence the Reformation in this country took on a form of its own, or had it imposed on it—a form which was in keeping with the political and social structure of the country and answered very tolerably to the character of the people. In the first place it was carried through by the King in consultation with Parliament. Henry shared responsibility with, and was in turn supported by, the effective political classes represented in the Lords and Commons. The great Reformation Parliament which was kept in session for the unprecedented period of six years (1529-35) put through the changes and gave them legislative form and sanction. It marked a constitutional stage of the greatest importance for the future place of Parliament in government. The supreme jurisdiction of the Papacy in all church matters was wholly renounced and its governing powers transferred to the Crown. The King became the head of an English national church. So far as power was concerned, the solution to the age-long conflicts between church and state was in England complete, logical, uncompromising. It was an absolute victory for the laity; the church was annexed to the state. But Henry had no wish to break with Catholic doctrine; that came later, and in a moderate form, full of compromise, yet having a character of its own.

There followed the dissolution of the monasteries throughout the country, the expropriation of the church not merely from monastic lands, but from a great deal of other property and much of its wealth. It is not too much to say that it was an economic revolution. Something like one-fifth of the whole land, and vast disposable wealth, came into the hands of the

Crown. A new department of state had to be set up to administer it; the operation of so gigantic a measure was a signal achievement of the administrative capacity of the new national state. Throughout the whole of this first phase of the Reformation, planning every step in co-ordination, supervising every administrative detail, Thomas Cromwell was in control: a political mind, clear, far-seeing, uncompromising, with a quality of revolutionary statesmanship like Lenin's—only this was a revolution of the rich.

The economic consequences of the Dissolution were indeed fundamental. In the first instance they operated to increase the power of the Crown. The wealth of the church was spent upon equipping the state with the instruments of power. Henry built a strong fleet, fortified the coasts, and waged yet another futile and expensive war with France (1543-6). To provide for the costs of government, which were mounting with the world-wide rise in prices due to American silver coming into Europe, the church lands were gradually sold off to the propertied classes. The process went on all through the century and into the next. The lands came to rest ultimately in the possession mainly of the country gentry, who worked them tenaciously and increased their productivity with the growing resources for capital investment. It meant an enormous increase in the wealth and power of the gentry—a tide which floated them to their onslaught on political power and the monarchy itself in the next century. But it also had the effect of stimulating productivity all round, in land, industry, and trade, and of producing the increase of wealth and economic energy which was at the bottom of the achievements of the Elizabethan Age.

Naturally these profound changes, which shook Europe like an earthquake and produced disturbances everywhere, of which the great Peasants' Revolt (1525-6) in Germany was the European example, were not without their repercussions

and parallels in England. The dissolution of the larger monasteries was held up by the Pilgrimage of Grace (1536-7), a
rising which held the northern counties in its grip and para-
lyzed Henry's government for many months. The King rose
to the occasion and by an artful combination of seduction,
political guile, and display of force overwhelmed the Catholic
north with a minimum of loss. The momentum for Henry's
forward policy came from London and the progressive southeast, from the gentry and the middle class. Opposition to the
new course from conservative elements, whether the old nobility or churchmen or peasants, was severely dealt with. Scions
of the oldest feudal families went to the block—a process that
continued all through the Tudor period. Nobody complained
much. The noblest exponent of the older ideal of the universal church, Sir Thomas More, among the greatest of Englishmen, died a martyr for the faith. It is good to record the
tribute of Dean Swift, so different a spirit, to More: 'the person of the greatest virtue that this kingdom hath ever produced.'

Henry VIII made an indomitable impression upon his people. He expressed in his personality the blustering growing
confidence of a young nation; he proclaimed and operated the
indivisible sovereignty of the new national state; he incor-
porated Wales into the framework of English government,
began the reorganization of Ireland, and united England of
the north with the progressive south. He died in the midst of
his plans for annexing Scotland to the English Crown. Here
he had been successfully thwarted by the independent party in
that country, supported by the French.

In the brief reign of his son Edward VI, the tempo of the
Reformation changes quickened. The Protestant oligarchy
around the boy king went on with the expropriation of church
lands hand in hand with the introduction of Protestant doctrine. An English Book of Common Prayer gave complete and

lasting expression to the national character of the reformed church. The new services were more congregational, with the emphasis on the people themselves instead of on the priest. This in the course of generations had its effect on their character, making them more active than passive—to use John Stuart Mill's classification of peoples. Individualism and private judgment were the essence of Protestantism. But it must be noticed that in England all the changes and reactions and forward moves were taken by the state itself; the process was guided and controlled by the central government so that the maximum of national uniformity was insisted upon and national unity retained, as against the fractionalizing tendencies that the Reformation encouraged in continental countries. Many of them emerged from it disunited, Germany chronically and disastrously so; England, because of the strength of the state, came through with its unity essentially unimpaired.

There were, however, local reactions in the outlying parts of the country. In 1549 there was a revolt among the Catholic peasantry of the west country against the new English Prayer Book. But it is significant that already the west-country seaports which were to play such a part in the Elizabethan Age were Protestant and forward-looking in sympathy. The profound disturbance of the old agrarian economy due to so many new factors, the European rise in prices, the debasing of the coinage, the change-over in ownership, enclosures and a more efficient exploitation of the land, led to another rising that convulsed East Anglia and some of the midland counties in the same year. The last rising of a feudal type on a big scale took place over the northern counties in 1569: it was led by the Northern Earls, who were Catholics and supporters of Mary Queen of Scots against Elizabeth. What is noticeable about all these risings, no less than those made by Protestants against Mary Tudor, is that they did not stand any real chance of success against the central government even though it had no standing army. Government in England was too securely founded, the state too strong for local anarchy to last long. In that a great contrast with France at this time, divided by religious war, and hence losing her place in the struggle for entry to the New World.

The most dangerous reaction in the forward movement that characterized the Tudor period was the reign of Mary (1553-8). The daughter of Catherine of Aragon, she was deeply religious and Catholic; her marriage to Philip II of Spain attached the country to the Spanish system of alliances and to Spanish interests, when it wished to be independent, to play for its own hand. Under Philip's rule English merchantmen were not allowed entry into the Spanish (or Portuguese) spheres of the New World, divided between them by the papal award. They were excluded as far as possible from the coasts of America and Africa, the Cape route to the East. It was very galling to national pride. At the same time the country was dragged into another war with France, which ended in the loss of Calais, the last remnant of our medieval conquests on the Continent. Mary and her cousin, Cardinal Pole, brought about England's formal return to the Roman fold; but it was a barren victory, for the laity kept the lands and wealth of the church. The hot pace of persecution which was set on foot against the Protestants only increased their number; while the burning of Archbishop Cranmer gave them a martyr to set beside the great Catholic, Sir Thomas More. The persecution was a fatal political mistake. Mary's régime was doomed before her death; she could not succeed against the vigorous young forces of the time; her supporters were old men, out of touch with the age; she herself was childless.

By a fortunate chance her successor Elizabeth was singularly well fitted both to express these new forces and to guide them through a hazardous and critical period: 'no elder statesman or famous captain in all broad Europe would have served so well to lead Englishmen back to harmony and prosperity and on to fresh fields of fame.' Hers was a subtle and brilliant Renaissance personality; she was young, but she was wise and something of a skeptic. She had been schooled in a hard and dangerous school of experience, the changes and chances, the currents and eddies of the Reformation. But she had great *joie de vivre*, tenacity of purpose beneath a thousand feminine changes of front—which moreover she exploited for her own ends—and a heroic spirit which held her on her course in spite of alarms and falterings. Hers was above all, beneath her more obvious gifts and talents, her knowledge of languages, her learning, her love of music and dancing, a political personality. She had a political genius, and it turned out that her reign was the most fortunate and the most glorious in our history: the Elizabethan Age.

From the outset (1558) she associated with herself the men of the new age, young like herself, in especial William Cecil, who remained as her chief minister at her side until five years from her own death in 1603. His son, Robert Cecil, continued the policy of his house until 1612: so that for more than a half-century the country was guided by one political dynasty, the most remarkable span of power that one family has exercised in our history, a formative influence of the first importance in the shaping of modern England. Mary's reign had marked the parting of the ways; her complete failure in every direction exposed the bankruptcy of the old order; the way was open for Elizabeth's new deal. In religion she returned to Edward VI's Protestant Prayer Book, broke with Rome, and re-established an independent national church. But for the rest, she was conservative and temporizing. She meant to keep as much national unity as was possible; for the first decade of her reign there was very little persecution. The internal organization of the church was left in its medieval form with a hierarchy of state-appointed bishops; doctrinally a good deal of scope was left for varying shades of belief, Catholic, Lutheran, Calvinist. It was a typical English compromise settlement, and through all the changes of centuries it has lasted ever since.

The keynote of Elizabeth's foreign policy was independence and a free hand for the expression of English national energies. For the first decade of her reign, in spite of her religious deviation, she kept on good terms with Philip, who did not wish to lose the English alliance or to allow England to fall into the Franco-Scottish orbit. Elizabeth began her reign with a great stroke of good fortune. In Scotland a Protestant national revolution, with the aid of English arms and an English fleet, forced the capitulation of the French forces which governed the country. From that time, in spite of the return of Mary Stuart to her realm and the difficulties that ensued, England had a friendly power upon her northern border instead of a hostile garrison in her rear whenever she went to war. It was a great turning-point, signaling the way to that union of the island which was the objective of so many centuries' policy and came about at Elizabeth's death and the accession of Mary Stuart's son, James I.

In the wider world of oceanic enterprise Elizabeth's reign marked an epoch in our history: the first steps were taken towards England's becoming a world power. The transition from medieval mediocrity was sudden, brilliant. It was due to the measure of unity and security achieved at home, behind the sea barrier

> Which serves it in the office of a wall,
> Or as a moat defensive to a house.

As early as the 1530's William Hawkins of Plymouth had made voyages to Brazil. His son, Sir John Hawkins, made trading expeditions along the Guinea coast for gold and slaves, then pushed across to enter the forbidden Caribbean and home by the coast of North America. In 1553 Chancellor explored along the north coast of Asia and entered the White Sea. He reached Moscow and began the trading contacts with Russia which bore fruit in the Muscovy Company. Anthony Jenkinson, the Company's agent, opened a land route to Persia and reached Bokhara. He was convinced that there was a sea route along the Siberian coast to the riches of the East. Another school of thought, of which Sir Humphry Gilbert, Frobisher, Davis were leaders, believed in the possibilities of a northwest route along the coast of Canada. Their efforts bore fruit in the colonization of Newfoundland, the discovery of Hudson's Bay, and, a century later (1670), the founding of the Hudson's Bay Company, which has played such a part in the story of Canada. Other merchants trading in the Mediterranean founded the Turkey Company in 1581, succeeded by the Levant Company in 1592; and, determined to share in the Portuguese monopoly of Far Eastern trade, started the East India Company, from which our Indian Empire grew. Its foundation was commerce, and for centuries, until the Industrial Revolution, the balance of trade was in India's favor.

But most important of all was the New World of America: for two centuries the chief efforts of English expansion were in the Atlantic. Gilbert was the first exponent of the idea of English colonization of North America. An idealist and projector himself, he inspired Sir Walter Ralegh and Grenville with his hopes and they planted the first English colony in Virginia, on Roanoke Island (1584-5). Then the long war with Spain held up our efforts for twenty years.

This war, which occupied the last two decades of Elizabeth's reign, was probably inevitable, though both Philip II and Elizabeth were pacific and did succeed in delaying war for years. But the underlying fact of the situation was the conflict for a share in the trade and possession of America. Spain and Portugal claimed a monopoly; and after 1580, when the Spanish and Portuguese Empires were united in Philip, England was confronted by a great danger. The whole of her future was at stake; she had to fight or consent to exclusion. It was this which brought on the war rather than religion; though that too was an element, and Philip supported the claims of Mary Stuart and the plots to assassinate Elizabeth to make way for her. Elizabeth retaliated by supporting the Dutch with arms and money, and eventually with armies and open aggression, in their national revolt against Spanish rule. She supported the Huguenot party similarly in its struggle against the Counter-Reformation and Spain raging upon French soil. In return Philip intervened in Ireland. Elizabeth was forced to undertake its conquest at great expense and the cost of infinite misery. This meant the beginning of the Irish national revolt against England.

Above all, and all the time, Elizabeth supported the activities of her seamen upon the oceans of the world. Hawkins' attempt to share with Spain in the trade of the Caribbean had been crushed in 1568: it was the end of the Anglo-Spanish alliance. Drake revenged Hawkins with incessant depredations upon the West Indies. Then he made the first English incursion into the Pacific, raiding the bullion route along the coast of Peru and returning home round the world. His career made an enormous impression upon his contemporaries, Englishmen and foreigners alike: they saw in him the daring spirit of a new country, a new age. When the long-simmering, unacknowledged conflict became open war, Drake took a famous part in it. He raided the West Indies, descended upon the coast of Spain, burnt Spanish shipping at Cadiz. Philip's reply was the Armada, a great fleet with the first army of Europe aboard. It was the crisis of English history.

Fortunately English shipbuilding and seamanship under Hawkins and Drake had reached the highest point they had yet attained. English ships, though smaller than the Spanish galleons, were swifter and more seaworthy and concentrated their gun-fire. They were the equivalent in 1588 of the Spitfires and Hurricanes which saved us in the Battle of Britain in 1940. The Spanish conception of sea warfare was Mediterranean: Spain was essentially a land power and conceived of her fleet as an army at sea. England was a sea power; ships and seamen were the essence of the matter to her. The meeting of these two conceptions in that memorable week in the Channel in July 1588 proved the superiority of the latter. The English fleet hung on, disorganizing the Armada, cutting off ships, and at length breaking its unity by the device of fire-ships off Calais. The Armada made for the North Sea and round Scotland and Ireland home to Spain; but not before storms and those coasts had destroyed more than half of the ships and the greater part of the men. It was a moment which our people have always remembered above all others in their history: henceforth England's future was in her own hands.

This was not the end of the war: it dragged on for almost twenty years with many ups and downs and strange chances. Next year Drake led a great expedition to Lisbon, which ended in a fiasco; later he and Hawkins went on their last expedition to the West Indies, upon which they both died, and were buried in those seas they knew so well; Sir Richard Grenville fought his last fight with Drake's old ship the *Revenge* in the Azores; Ralegh led his expedition to Guiana in the hope of founding an English empire in South America; Cavendish followed Drake in his track round the world; Philip dispatched another Armada which was driven back by storms at the entrance to the Channel. But in fact the issue of the war was settled, though peace was not made until Philip and Elizabeth were both dead, and then nothing was said about the real issue. What was really decided by the long struggle, the first of our modern oceanic wars, was that North America was to be open to English colonization: a determining event in world history and for our own fate as a people. The question of English trade with South America was left unsettled, the fruitful seed of future wars, until the gaining of their independence by the Southern and Central American states decided it in their own interests.

To what did England owe her astonishing success in the long duel? It is not easy to explain it, for the balance of power on the other side, a dominant position in Europe, a world empire, was overwhelming. It would seem to have been mainly due to the social flexibility, the adaptability, the modernity of the English state. It had no caste system such as prevented the nobility on the Continent from taking part in commerce. We were more like Holland: merchants and mariners had a high place in the national esteem. And rightly, for we owed our fortunes to them. The Tudors were very sensitive to the claims, and the rewards, of commerce. Elizabeth, like Henry VII, did not make the mistake of straining the national resources: she did what she did with an elegant economy. Her glorious meanness deserves to be inscribed in letters of gold upon the annals of her people; for it was their salvation. They were a small people, and not rich as peoples go.

Their emergence from such a time of testing had the effect of release and inspiration such as Athens experienced after the Persian War, by which she created that miracle of the European mind. The Elizabethan was, and always will be, our Golden Age. The English speech flowered suddenly into the magnificence of great literature. The mood became one of a released and soaring confidence. 'Look! We have come through!' the poets seem to say, expressing the mind of the nation. In the years immediately after the Armada the Elizabethan drama springs into life and starts on its triumphant course. Marlowe and the early Shakespeare express this mood of transcendent confidence and national spirit; especially Marlowe, whose genius was made of intellectual pride and the

Renaissance lust for beauty and power: dead at twenty-seven in a tavern brawl—but not before he had written a masterpiece and much imperishable poetry. Shakespeare was a gentler and more English spirit, in whom the English people see themselves reflected as in a mirror: at his very heart was a dream of the English countryside, of Puck and Queen Mab, of fairies and hob-goblins. He made a play out of it all and called it *A Midsummer Night's Dream.* And at the end of his intense and crowded life in London, the vivacious and electric London of Elizabeth, full of courtiers, merchants, mariners, shopkeepers, apprentices, rogues, adventurers, he turned back to his dream and wrote *The Tempest.*

> Be not afeared: the isle is full of noises,
> Sounds and sweet airs, that give delight, and hurt not.
> Sometimes a thousand twangling instruments
> Will hum about mine ears; and sometime voices,
> That, if I then had waked after long sleep,
> Will make me sleep again: and then in dreaming,
> The clouds methought would open and show riches
> Ready to drop upon me; that when I waked
> I cried to dream again.

It might be a dream of the age of Elizabeth, for England too was a land of music then.

Shakespeare's extraordinary sensitiveness made him a subtler and more sympathetic interpreter of the various moods of the age than the more wilful and intellectual Marlowe. And so he ended by creating a whole world of the imagination, a realm of the human spirit which mirrors the English Renaissance at its best. Spenser and Sir Philip Sidney looked to the past; but they too were men of the Renaissance aware of the contemporary artistic achievements of Italy, France, Spain, and determined to make English poetry great as theirs was. They succeeded: there was never a more creative epoch in any modern literature. It is impossible to do justice to the poets or the prose-writers, the writers of songs or the dramatists here, they were so many: Drayton, Ben Jonson, Campion, Hakluyt, Ralegh, Donne, Webster, Beaumont and Fletcher, Nashe, Dekker, Ford. The translators rendered in their golden English the riches of foreign literature both ancient and modern, from Latin, Greek, Italian, French, Spanish: it is a whole literature of its own and we can mention no more than the pre-eminent among them—Chapman, the translator of Homer, for poetry; in prose North, Florio, Philemon Holland, 'translator-general of the age.' In Francis Bacon the age had one of its greatest luminaries: a foremost figure in the development of modern science and philosophy, a great lawyer, a master of prose. A no less great prose-writer was Richard Hooker, who in his *Laws of Ecclesiastical Polity* formulated the intellectual position of the English church, an enduring monument. No such master of prose as these but a lawyer of the greatest importance was Coke, exponent and defender of the Common Law against both Roman Law and royal prerogative. His *Reports* and *Institutes* mark the dividing line between the Middle Ages and modern English law, which was to have such a prodigious future before it in America, the Dominions, India, the Empire: an extension comparable only to that of Roman Law itself.

Nor were there wanting scientists, like Harriott the mathematician and Dr. Dee the geographer, who, himself a Welshman, invented the phrase the 'British Empire.' Only a little later came the great William Harvey, discoverer of the circulation of the blood. In music it was the age of William Byrd, greatest of our composers, compeer of Palestrina, and of many another lesser star, Tallis, Morley, Weelkes, Orlando Gibbons. Europe recognized Elizabethan England as a most musical country, where the spirit of the people expressed itself richly and variously in a fine tradition of music. Nor in architecture were they far behind: the Elizabethan was the first great period in our domestic architecture. The new wealth opened out by the Reformation changes on the land, by trade and commerce at home and beyond the seas, found outlet in innumerable mansions in the country and in town houses, of which enough remain today to give us an idea of the elegance and dignity of the life lived by our forefathers under those roofs. Their very style expresses the instinctive compromise between medieval and Renaissance, gothic and classical, between the splendid and the homely, which they had attained; and withal, there is something very English about it.

These things, like much in our institutions, express an adaptation of our own that we have been able to make as the result of a continuous security: 'a privilege usually confined to countries either very humble or very remote, but enjoyed in this case by a Great Power on the very highway of the world's affairs. . . Its first good gift was the rich harvest of the Elizabethan Renaissance.'

IV. Revolutionary England

NEARLY all great countries, except Germany, have undergone a revolution: England included. People are apt to think of English history as a conservative affair, when it has been the most dynamic and inwardly changing of any country. In recent times foreigners have noticed the conservative character of our institutions and inferred that as a people we are opposed to change. But in the seventeenth century they regarded us very differently: we were then thought to be the most restless, turbulent, and changeable of peoples. And with some reason: a nation that in the course of half a century underwent two revolutions, two civil wars and narrowly escaped another, executed one king and sent another packing, tried a Parliamentary Republic and a military Protectorate before arriving at a mixed constitution of its own making—such a country can hardly be accused of dullness or placidity.

The fact is that this country too has had its revolutionary past, like France from 1789, Russia from 1917; only our revolution took place in the seventeenth century. It exercised a very great influence upon Europe for the next century, until the French Revolution. Its effect at home was ultimately to create a political system and institutions capable of evolving further change, broadening the basis of power, and enabling the people to share in liberty. So that since the seventeenth century, revolutionary changes have been able to take place within English society without any further breach of constitutional continuity. That is the paradox of outward conservatism with the inner capacity for development which lies at the heart of modern England. And therein lies the peculiarity of our history: it goes back to the seventeenth century, in the course of which, by a series of revolutionary changes, we took a different development from that abroad and set out on a course of our own. We ended up the century with a system of parliamentary government, voluntary local administration, and freedom of speech and person, as against the prevailing tendencies on the continent towards absolutism, bureaucracy, centralization, and the subjection of the individual to the state.

We have seen that, through the dangerous period of the Reformation and Counter-Reformation, a remarkable degree of unity was maintained in this country. Its visible embodiment was the Crown, the Tudor monarchy. All classes in the community were united in respect and obedience to that resplendent symbol; the Crown was the source of effective political power at the center; government was in its hands and those of its executive instrument, the Council. That unity and that form were maintained so long as danger threatened from abroad and the war with Spain continued.

The accession of James I brought peace at home and abroad; and peace was maintained throughout his reign. It was a great boon, after a generation of war and decades of high tension. The century-long feuds which had troubled the Anglo-Scottish Border, the wars which had often devastated the Scottish Lowlands or the English Border and constituted such a distraction to our policy, came to an end. The union of the two kingdoms was achieved by the better way of the smaller providing a dynasty for the greater: very satisfactory to the pride of both parties. The cessation of the Spanish War, with its cumulative financial drain, released economic energies and wealth for investment. The war in Ireland came to an end with the plantation of Ulster with hard-working, hard-bitten Scottish Protestants: an act of colonization which henceforth was a factor of the first importance in Anglo-Irish relations and in the history of that country. The Jacobean peace enabled England to advance in wealth by leaps and bounds.

It was now that the country took advantage of the great opportunities which the Elizabethans had fought for. In 1609 the first permanent English colony was founded in America at Jamestown. From then on, between the Spanish War and the Civil War, the Atlantic colonies were founded. Hardly less important was the movement into the West Indies, beginning with the Bermudas and going down the chain of the outer Caribbean Islands to Ralegh's Guiana. In these decades there was a spontaneous swarming-off of colonists from the old country to the new such as had never occurred before and has since only occurred once, in the early and middle nineteenth century. The merchants provided capital, the gentry leaders; but it was the husbandmen, tillers of the soil, whose solid man-power made the foundation of the American colonies, and all that future. It was now that the East India Company first sent out its regular expeditions of well-armed trading ships which won an increasing share in the rich trade of the East Indies, against the Portuguese and in competition with the Dutch. The founding of an English trading post at Surat was the first step towards the making of the Indian Empire. It was then too that we made a move that led in the end to the African Empire: a settlement on the Gambia and the setting-up of the Africa Company (1618).

These efforts were the natural expression of the vigorous energies of a newly-arrived and successful nation. The incompetent government of the Stuarts hindered rather than helped; their neglect of the Elizabethan navy meant that English traders had to fight in distant lands for their own hand— which they were fortunately well able to do. But not unnaturally the Stuarts were rewarded with unpopularity among merchants and mariners, in the seaports and in the navy, and with their active hostility in the Civil War. At home, the increase of wealth was to be seen in the growing scale and number of the great houses being built over the countryside, the ostentation of the court and aristocracy, the affluence of gentry and merchants, the vulgar magnificence of Jacobean society.

Actually, under the surface of the old political forms, a profound change in the balance of social forces was getting under way in the last decades of Elizabeth. This was the beginning of the upward movement in the fortunes and power of the gentry which encroached upon the preserves of the Crown, nobility, and peasantry alike, and ended by changing the balance of English society in the course of the century. It was the fundamental social force from which the seventeenth-century Revolution sprang. Already before Elizabeth's death, the House of Commons were staking their claim to have a say in government. They developed the technique of Committees by which to gather business into their hands and dispatch it efficiently. Under James and Charles these tendencies were pushed all along the line. The Commons were the innovators, reaching out for a share in political power which corresponded to their immense acquisitions in economic power. The Crown, whose financial resources were shrinking all the time, with most of the church lands sold, and incapable of meeting the expenses of government, was reduced to the defensive. Such was the essence of the situation that led to the Civil War and Revolution, though it was complicated by other factors, personal and religious.

So long as James lived, he did well enough, and the struggle did not come to an irremediable breach. Though personally tactless, he was politically shrewd; and in a way his reign may be regarded as an aftermath of Elizabeth's, with something of the sun's afterglow upon it. Until 1612 government was in the hands of Robert Cecil, who continued his father's policies with his father's wisdom and sureness of touch. But at the outset of his reign, at the Hampton Court Conference, James missed an opportunity of securing comprehension within the framework of the national church for the Puritan clergy. They were driven outside: they provided spiritual leadership and a doctrine for the more uncompromising gentry of Puritan sympathies: Puritanism was their ideology. They became the nucleus of the great body of Dissent from which sprang the rich variety of Nonconformity, with its diverse contributions to the spiritual and intellectual life of the nation.

As some compensation for this failure, however, James's bishops gave us the Authorized Version of the Bible (1604-11). It seems hardly less than a miracle that a committee of ecclesiastics should have produced an undying masterpiece of English prose: tribute to the bloom and perfection of Elizabethan language and the imaginative richness of the time. 'The effect of the continual domestic study of the book upon the national character, imagination and intelligence for nearly three centuries to come, was greater than any literary movement in our annals, or any religious movement since the coming of St. Augustine.' The Book opened up a whole new world of history, imagination, poetry, belief, perhaps as influential in the mind of the English people as the Renaissance itself.

The greatest intellect of the age, Francis Bacon, was set in favor of a wider degree of toleration, and he had some influence with James in his later years. But the sympathies of Charles I were altogether narrower; a man of taste and personal uprightness, he was very deficient in what Elizabeth possessed to her finger-tips, political sense, tact, judgment. He soon involved himself in a series of quarrels with Parliament over finance and policy, which culminated in a defeat for the King at the hands of the Commons and their leader, Sir John Eliot. The King decided to rule without Parliament and for eleven years he did so, relying mainly upon Laud as his adviser in church and state, and Strafford as his executive in the north and later in Ireland. This meant that the monarchy, without grants of money from Parliament, had to strain its resources and its rights to get the wherewithal to carry on government, incurring the odium of the gentry; while in foreign affairs Britain was reduced to a cipher.

Laud was a High Churchman, determined to push the claims and prerogatives of the church and Crown in every corner of national life: Archbishop of Canterbury, the last ecclesiastic to govern the country, dogged, tenacious, out of touch with the age, in the end a martyr to his cause. Strafford was a great man who watched the absolutist tendencies of the time abroad and wished to found a strong monarchy based upon an army and an efficient administration. He too was going against the current of social forces in this country and was tragically aware of it; he came to full power too late, just in time to be struck down by them, a victim to his own class, the gentry in full cry after power. In the interval he had governed the north efficiently and with justice; and had given Ireland an example of able, strong, just government, bringing order out of chaos, the beginnings of a modern state.

The future was not with him, but with his social class. In the absence of Parliament, which had become their instrument, they resisted the King at every point through their law courts and their lawyers, the Common Law. Charles's attempt to raise money to bring up the strength of the neglected fleet was met with a moral defeat inflicted upon him by John Hampden, in the famous Ship Money case. But it was Charles's and Laud's ill-considered design to force their religious policy, episcopacy, and the English Prayer Book upon Scotland that gave the gentry their opportunity. The Scots reacted with a national revolt, which was led by the Kirk (the Church) and expressed itself in the form of a religious Covenant, because the organs of political life were lacking. Poor, hardy, armed, they easily raised an army which invaded

England. The King of his own could raise no adequate resistance to them; their demand for money forced him to call Parliament. And so the Scottish revolt of 1638-40 began the British Revolution.

In 1640 there met the Long Parliament which was the 'true turning-point in the political history of the English-speaking races.' The leadership in the events which followed was taken by a great revolutionary statesman, John Pym. He led the Commons in their attack upon the prerogatives of Crown and church, the system of government for which Charles, Laud, and Strafford stood. The Star Chamber, the Court of High Commission, the royal Councils which had directly governed the north and Wales were abolished. Strafford, ablest of Charles's advisers, who might yet have saved him, was executed. The King was forced to assent to a measure which forbade the dissolution of Parliament without its own consent—evidence of how vital Parliament was to the gentry as their political instrument. So far Pym had led them unitedly. But he perceived, like Strafford on the other side, that such a balance in government between Crown and Parliament could not be maintained and that it was necessary to go further. He took the revolutionary road of parliamentary government: he forced through the Grand Remonstrance which meant that ministers should be responsible to Parliament—from which it was but a step to Parliament making them—and a measure for reconstructing the church on Parliamentarian principles. On these revolutionary changes the Commons split: the majority following Pym, the minority which was opposed to revolution forming a party for the King and church. No compromise was possible in this struggle for power. Such were the two parties whose conflict broke out into the great Civil War.

Behind Parliament were ranged London with its inexhaustible resources of wealth and trade, most of the towns with their commercially-minded and Puritan middle class, the sea-ports and the progressive part of the country, the east and south. Behind the King were ranged the old feudal magnates, the Catholics and the church, the old-fashioned squires and peasantry of the north and west. London and its wealth were a decisive factor in the war. With its control of the sea and of trade Parliament was in a position to organize the long-run financing of the war; in the devices it worked out for this purpose we find the germ of our modern fiscal system. In the end its economic resources were too much for the Royalists; the King lost the war for want of money.

With so much stronger resources Parliament ought to have won the war early, if it could have turned them into imme-diate assets. But the Royalists were more accustomed to arms and in the first year had the advantage not only in Prince Rupert's cavalry but in the magnificent infantry which the Cornish peasantry made. The Royalist victories of 1643 made the situation look black for Parliament, when Pym achieved his last act of high statesmanship by making an alliance with the Scots and bringing their army in on the side of Parlia-ment. He died shortly after, but nevertheless he was the architect of Parliamentarian victory. Meanwhile Parliament financed a new regular army under its direct service, with good long-term conditions and under strict discipline: Oliver Cromwell's New Model.

Cromwell was an East Anglian squire who in the course of the war developed both military and political gifts of the highest order. As a master of cavalry tactics he became the superior of Prince Rupert, from whom he learned. The first fruit of Pym's Scottish alliance and the New Model army was the shattering defeat of the Royalists in 1644 at Marston Moor, the greatest battle of the war. It was followed next year by Naseby, when the King was driven out of the field. After these disasters—in which Cromwell's Ironsides from East

Anglia bore the decisive part—the Royalist cause quickly broke up in Wales and the west country where support for it was strongest. Though the war had been fought all through with a high standard of honor and chivalry on both sides, after four years of it men were anxious to come to terms with the obviously stronger side and return to peace and security. Parliament had a great opportunity before it.

If Pym had lived it is conceivable that he would have given the country the civilian settlement it needed—he had a great insight into political realities and the prestige of his leadership would have been immense—and there would have been no dictatorship of Cromwell and the army. Without Pym's leadership Parliament threw away in three years the great opportunity that was there for a permanent settlement. In its defense, it may be said, there was the enormous difficulty in shaping a new course untried in so short a time. In short the political and constitutional problems involved in the Revolution took the rest of the century to work out and duly achieved a satisfactory working solution with the settlement after the Revolution of 1688. The combination of forces which had won the Civil War was not strong enough to appropriate power to itself alone and conduct the government against the rest of the country. Still less were the moneyed squires and business men of London, who were the core of the Parliamentarians, strong enough to rule against both the Royalists and Cromwell's army, which had won the victory for them. Yet that is what they tried to do: the rule of a narrow oligarchical clique.

The Puritans of the Long Parliament turned out to be more intolerant than anybody else—far more so than the Church of England—and they were less representative of the nation. To meet the financial cost of the war they attacked the property of their opponents. And so instead of reconciling themselves to the régime in return for security, the squires

THE CIVIL WAR 1643

SCOTLAND

Dunbar ×
Edinburgh

ROYALIST

Marston Moor × York
Hull

R. Trent

ROYALIST PARLIAMENTARIAN

R. Severn
Naseby
×
Worcester × Cambridge
× Edgehill
Gloucester Oxford
London
Bristol R. Thames

ROYALIST
Exeter

Plymouth

Miles

0   50   100   150

Battles... ×

Stanford, London.

conceived a very natural loathing for Puritanism. Puritan confiscations cemented a political alliance between squire and parson, gentry and church, which persisted through the Revolution of 1688 and the eighteenth century into the nineteenth and up to our own time. Not content with this, Parliament, egged on by the City of London, quarreled with the army and refused to pay its arrears. This was more immediately dangerous. The army retaliated by coercing Parliament, purging it of its political opponents. It was the first step to Cromwell's dictatorship.

The balance lay now in the hands of the defeated King. The army offered him very reasonable terms, a wide measure of religious toleration, a stop to confiscation, a sharing of power. But Charles could not conceive of any other than monarchical government; he played at negotiating with the army leaders while secretly allying himself with Parliament in the hope of restoring his own power. This alliance led to the Second Civil War and the rapid victory of Cromwell. The army leaders brought the King to book and executed him at Whitehall in 1649.

The execution of the King marked the consummation of the revolution. It administered a profound shock to the country; henceforth there was no turning back for the revolutionary leaders. They had need of all their resources of courage and ability to draw the country out of chaos, or indeed to govern at all in such a divided land. But the very circumstances of revolution brought to the top, as revolution does, unexpected reserves of ability, men of great natural powers of courage and leadership. The Commonwealth proved an era of great public servants the like of which England had not known since the days of Elizabeth. Cromwell showed himself to have powers of political leadership not inferior to his military genius; Blake was one of our greatest naval commanders; the Republic was well served by Milton, Vane, Ireton, Monk,

Thurloe, Marvell. (We may disregard the disagreeable religious enthusiasm which the times engendered and which their exigencies, perhaps, demanded.) In three years they had drawn order out of chaos, united England, Scotland and Ireland in a strong legislative and economic union, and made the name of the Republic feared and respected abroad.

Ireland was first subjugated by Cromwell and Ireton (1649-50); after its conquest the ownership of the soil was transferred on a large scale to Cromwellian soldiers, the Catholic Irish expropriated or pushed beyond the Shannon. Such was the effective foundation of the rule of the Anglo-Irish which continued economically till the end of the nineteenth century and politically until the founding of the Irish Free State in 1922. Next the Scots were defeated at Dunbar and Worcester. Then the Commonwealth took the naval situation in hand: 'their measures transformed the Navy to its modern scope and established England as the great naval power of the world.' Blake swept the Royalists off the seas and first took British naval power into the Mediterranean, where it has ever since been: an important factor in world history. The Navigation Act of 1651 marked the revival of English commercial power and her determination to increase her share of the carrying trade. It led to the first Dutch War, the first phase in the struggle against Dutch maritime supremacy (1652-4).

But Cromwell desired Protestant co-operation in Europe and preferred to continue the Elizabethan quarrel with Spain. Like Pym he was an imperialist: he sent an expedition to the West Indies which captured Jamaica, the biggest step yet taken in building up that West Indian Empire which held such a key position in trade and war henceforward. Still, Cromwell's militant imperialism gained increasing unpopularity, especially among the mercantile classes, on account of its cost. So long as the great Protector lived and maintained control of the army, he could continue to govern even against the balance of social forces in the country. But when he died the different sections of the propertied classes, Royalist and Parliamentarian landowners, the business men of the city, were brought together by the fear of social anarchy and the radicalism of the lower orders and their sects. They joined together to form an alliance upon which to bring about a restoration of the King on their terms. The pivot in this turn was Monk at the head of the army, himself connected with both parties in the landowning class, Royalists and Parliamentarians.

Upon this foundation Charles II came back, with his gay French court, but guided politically by Clarendon, the man of 1641. It was the end of the rule of the Saints, of high seriousness and Republican virtue. The greatest poet of the age, John Milton, his eyes put out by the work he had done in the service of the Republic, dedicated himself to that great epic of defeat, *Paradise Lost,* with which, like Dante, he consoled himself for loss of power, the ruin of his hopes. The Puritan *débâcle* meant that England was to become less democratic, more aristocratic and oligarchical; meant also that we lost touch with Puritan New England across the seas, which became increasingly independent in spirit. At home the tone of the age was one of enjoyment, brilliance, release after repression. Court and theater, music, and the arts bloomed after so austere, so invigorating a winter. When London burned in the Great Fire, it was rebuilt in stone on a much more handsome scale within a few years; opportunity for the deployment of the genius of Sir Christopher Wren, greatest of our architects, who built St. Paul's Cathedral, many City churches, buildings at Oxford and Cambridge, and designed a number of royal palaces.

Not only the arts but the sciences flourished and achieved a brilliant fruition with the founding of the Royal Society, of which Sir Isaac Newton was the chief ornament, supreme in his mathematical discoveries, his formulation of new laws of the physical universe. He was not alone: there were such prolific inventors as Hooke and Boyle, and later the astronomer Halley. The morose intellectual genius of Hobbes had penetrated the facts of power which underlie society with his *Leviathan:* the chief contribution of the revolutionary age to political thought, a work which puts him on a par with Machiavelli. The disturbed times produced a flood of political speculation and some very distinguished thinkers; until the Revolution of 1688 found its exponent and philosopher in Locke, most English of political thinkers, defender of toleration and compromise, founder of classical economics, ancestor of English Liberalism: the most potent intellectual influence for the next century.

The intellectual activity reflected the agitation of the age; the richness of the arts, the increase of wealth that continued at a heightened pace all through the Restoration period. The Commonwealth confiscations of Royalist property added a new element to the landed gentry, which became a strand in the Whig party. But the economic movement of the time was towards larger agglomerations of property, greater accumulations of wealth. This meant increasing concentration of political power in the hands of a small number of great potentates: it was they who directed the Revolution of 1688 and governed the country for a century and a half after it. Throughout Charles II's reign the East India Company enjoyed an unparalleled prosperity: the wealth of that trade was becoming a factor in politics. The West Indies and America yielded increasing returns; especially after the second Dutch war ended in adding the Middle American Colonies to the Empire, with the great commercial center which became New York. By the end of the century England was the greatest manufacturing and trading country in the world, and London had taken the place of Amsterdam as Europe's chief emporium.

Brilliant as was the society of the Restoration, its achievements in the arts, in science, and economic progress, the period was unsatisfactory and disappointing politically. The root of the trouble lay in the unresolved conflict for power between the two great interests in the state, the large mass of the conservative smaller gentry, who were ranged mostly behind the King and the church and became the Tory party, and the socially more progressive interests of the great Whig potentates and their allies in business and trade and industry, with their outlying offshoots in Dissent. Until the magnates won their victory in 1688, it was impossible for England to give Europe that leadership against the aggressive power of Louis XIV which her position and her interests demanded. The struggle between Crown and Parliament was but the political expression of this underlying conflict.

The compromise between parties which effected Charles II's Restoration attempted to restore the balance between Crown and Parliament in the work of government which the Long Parliament had arrived at in 1641. The legislation of that year remained untouched after the floods had subsided. But in the interval, the Commonwealth had given an unforgettable example of unified control and national power. One thing the Revolution had settled for good and all: that the government of the country could never again be conducted against the will of the classes represented in Parliament. But under Charles II and James II there was nevertheless a ceaseless struggle between Crown and Parliament as to which was to have the larger say. In the conflict the real interests of the state suffered serious damage: the country ceased to fulfil its proper role in European affairs; it lost the prestige it had enjoyed under the great Protector and Elizabeth. It is not too much to say that the later Stuarts sold the interests of the country to Louis XIV, whose power in consequence grew into a danger to the independence of other European states. For this betrayal of the interests of the country and of Europe the Stuarts earned a well-merited retribution: exile and that fatal family's long faltering decay, pensionaries first of Louis XIV and then of the Hanoverians who supplanted them in England.

This is the clue to the instability, the feverish party activity of 1660-88. Parliament would not grant Charles II enough money to govern efficiently, for fear of his becoming independent. This was the reason for the humiliations of the second Dutch war, when the Dutch burnt English warships laid up in the Medway. In consequence Charles turned to Louis for money in return for a joint campaign against Holland and a Catholic policy in England. This led to Louis' invasion of Holland in 1672 and the most terrible threat to Dutch independence, which they only survived by the greatest fighting qualities and fortitude. The danger suddenly revealed to the English people that their maritime rivalry with Holland was less important than the threat of Louis XIV to their very security and the freedom of Europe if the Netherlands came under the domination of France. Holland saved herself and Europe by her exertions. The reaction in England enabled Danby to befriend her and to carry through that dynastic alliance between Mary, the ultimate heiress to the English throne, and William of Orange, which bore fruit in the Revolution settlement of 1688.

The underlying conflict for power was reflected in the religious sphere, where the Restoration failed, as the Commonwealth had done, to bring about toleration. The triumphant Royalists would allow no more toleration to the Dissenters than these had been willing to extend to Anglicans in their day of power. Very human; very foolish. Both sides refused to learn that the only solution in the interest of the country was mutual toleration of the other's vagaries. Only the philo-sophically-minded, like Halifax or Locke, or the skeptical, like Charles or Shaftesbury, could be expected to see that. But the excesses, and the disagreeable enthusiasms, of both sides gradually made way in more adult minds for the age of reason and common sense. The Tory squires of the Restora-tion forced through a series of measures excluding Dissenters from sharing in the power and amenities of society, barring them from education and weighing them down with disabili-ties. Charles and James, who were both engaged in a cam-paign, the one surreptitiously, the other openly, to favor Ca-tholicism, tried to suspend the laws against the Dissenters. This led to prolonged struggles with Parliament, for it raised again in an acute form the whole question of the royal pre-rogative and how far the Crown might suspend the operation of the laws of the country. On this question turned the consti-tutional struggles that raged fiercely in these years, out of which our historic parties, Whigs and Tories, were formed.

So long as Charles II lived, his tact and political sense pre-vented an irreparable breach. But James II was without either; and moreover he was a fervent Catholic determined to foist his beliefs upon a Protestant country. The Whigs, in a fierce and unscrupulous campaign, had tried to exclude him from the throne. The moderate Tories, looking to the succession after him of Mary and William, saved him. On becoming king he rewarded them with Stuart ingratitude. He used the pitiable failure of Monmouth's rebellion to maintain a stand-ing army on Louis XIV's money, with which to overawe London. He was determined both to erect a despotism on a military basis and to force his religious designs, against the advice of the old Catholic nobility, upon an alienated people. In three years he had antagonized practically every section of his supporters. His very attempt showed that politically he was a fool of the first water, for it left him completely isolated to face a coalition of Whigs and Tories, landowners and moneyed men, Church and Dissent. It was impossible for him to make way against the overwhelming forces he had united against him: they gave him enough rope to hang himself and then called in William of Orange. James fled.

It was practically a bloodless revolution. The struggle was yet to come with Louis XIV. For with the Revolution England moved into that position of natural leadership against his aggressive designs in Europe which the paralyzing conflict for power within the country had prevented it from taking. Louis XIV had taken advantage of our being a mere counter in Europe under the Stuarts to build up an overwhelming ascendancy which threatened the independence of Holland and the German States, the safety of everybody else in western Europe. The result was that it took nearly twenty years of war to defeat him. The necessary precondition of his defeat was the alliance between England and Holland, formerly rivals. The accession of Dutch William to the English throne clinched that alliance in the most effective way possible; it gave him the power, which his courage and political genius exploited to the full, to organize the great European coalition which checked Louis in full flight and finally brought him to defeat.

At home it was a great blessing that James II's mistakes and follies had united the aristocracy, and indeed all classes, against him. For it meant that though party conflict was not extinguished but continued at high pitch for twenty years, until the Hanoverian succession, yet the Revolution was achieved with the maximum of national unity: both Whigs and Tories were party to it. The aristocracy had won: the long rivalry between Crown and Parliament gave way to a partnership in which Parliament, as the political instrument of the aristocracy, was indubitably stronger. The Crown itself rested upon a parliamentary title; and in 1701 the Act of

Settlement vested the succession to the throne, after William and Anne, in the Protestant House of Hanover. Yet the English monarchy was no mere doge-ship, the state was not a crowned republic: the Crown retained the powers of executive government, but by the terms of the Revolution settlement could never again use them against Parliament. It was in part the accident of three weak sovereigns in succession, two of whom were foreigners imperfectly acquainted with the English language, which helped to transfer the executive powers of the Crown to Parliament. After a pattern of our own, we were in the way of becoming a constitutional monarchy.

For the rest, the Revolution was a conservative one, with liberal intentions partly fulfilled. In the sphere of religion the Restoration settlement of 1660 was not essentially disturbed: the Church of England was left in its privileged position as the established state church. The promises to the Nonconformists were honored in the Toleration Act of 1689, by which they were accorded the right to public worship in their own forms, but remained excluded from political and social privilege. But the whole intellectual trend both within and without the church was set towards toleration and reasonableness: the first of the good products of an aristocratic age. After the doctrinal and party ardors and excitements of the seventeenth century, men were prepared to welcome the rule of common sense, reason, and moderation. Locke presided in dignified fashion over men's minds, and he pointed the way to the skeptical toleration of Hoadley, the skeptical idealism of Berkeley, the skepticism and sense of Hume and Gibbon, greatest of English philosophers and historians: the gods of a new age.

This mixed settlement was made by a number of not very noble, but very clever men. It proved itself singularly well suited to the circumstances in which the country found itself in the new century: the commercial and maritime expansion at home and abroad, the growth of industry and capital, of the colonies, rivalry with France in Europe, America, India, war. It released energies which had gone too much into internal conflict and gave them a chance to deploy themselves in the interest of the nation: England turned her attention abroad once more. Surely a fortunate settlement to which so many agreed; for almost immediately the Revolution was plunged into a life and death struggle with Louis XIV. In the year 1690 Ireland was the pivot of the European crisis. The Irish had taken advantage of James's sympathies to reverse the Cromwellian settlement and restore power to the Catholic landowners. With French arms and money, James landed in Ireland to continue the double struggle of the Irish against the English, French domination against the European coalition. The Protestant garrison in Ulster proved its effectiveness, holding out until William arrived with his Anglo-Dutch army to defeat James at the Boyne and drive him from the country. The Protestant settlement was re-imposed; Ireland was once more sacrificed to the exigencies of European politics. And not merely the Catholic Irish; the Protestant interest—the cloth trade, the export of cattle—was no less sacrificed to English commercial interests in the ensuing century.

The Revolution settlement in Scotland provides a happier picture. The Scots took the opportunity to reverse the religious policy of the Stuarts and to establish Presbyterianism as the state church. Their virtual independence gave them great bargaining power in negotiating the Act of Union with which the Revolution settlement was completed. This brought into being an economic and political union between England and Scotland. Scotland sent members to the British Parliament; England opened her home and colonial markets to Scottish industry and agriculture; the Scots became participators in

English enterprise in the outside world. Though something of nationhood may have been lost, Scotland began at once to prosper, and not merely economically. The soil of her mind bore fruit more abundantly, no less than the soil itself: the age of Hume, Adam Smith, Burns, Scott, was the greatest in her intellectual life. Scotland soon began to make a contribution to every aspect of British life, literature, administration, in war and empire, out of all proportion to her size and numbers. There can be no denying that the Revolution settlement had a great success with the Union: where before was conflict and repression was now release, co-operation, achievement.

Louis had built up a great fleet which was superior to both the English and the Dutch in the first years of the war. Yet he made no effective use of it. The turning-point of the war came with our great sea-victory off La Hogue in 1692, as decisive in its way as Trafalgar in 1805. After it William could carry the war into the offensive across the seas, and, fighting on all the frontiers his aggressions had threatened, Louis was unable to keep his fleet up to strength. The war went on for years and Louis was forced on the defensive. It was no strain upon the resilient resources of united Britain. The moneyed classes lent their money—the increase of trade and industry made it possible; the new institution of the Bank of England provided an easy technique. The economy of the country was singularly well-balanced, mainly agricultural with an increasing productivity. The accumulation of capital was being more effectively applied to developing the resources of the country. The English people were prospering; there was a sound and progressive relation of social forces. Where France or Prussia had a large class of serfs upon the land, in England there was a very substantial class of yeomen or tenant farmers.

A marked contrast economically as well as politically prevailed between France and Great Britain, the two great protagonists in the struggle that filled the next century. France was much larger, with three times the population. Yet the advantages were not all on one side. 'England with its greater resources of practicable coal and metals, with its growing overseas commerce and with its changing agrarian life underwent an "industrial revolution." France did not. While in France therefore regulation by the state increased in extent and effectiveness, in England apprenticeship, gild control and the other defenses of the small enterprise all gave way before private initiative.' The achievements of the next two centuries were to an extraordinary degree those of private initiative, free enterprise: their astonishing record of success, their prestige, were partly responsible for making the English adhere to them into our own time when, perhaps, other methods and combinations were called for.

The strain of the long war with France bore most hardly on the Dutch, whose resources, of the three powers, were most limited. In the course of the war England developed hers and outpassed the Dutch. Yet how much we owed to Dutch influence in this, the greatest age in their history; how much we learned from them in the spheres of administration, finance, business, shipping. And not these alone. In literature and the arts the chief influences upon this country came, as in previous ages, largely from France and Italy. But now Dutch gardens became the fashion, Dutch painting provided an important influence upon the subsequent school of English landscape painting; London learned its banking methods from Amsterdam; there was much intellectual intercourse between England and Holland. We owed our salvation to a Dutchman —one of the greatest in the long line of our kings.

V. Commerce and Empire

THE settlement of the internal conflict for power enabled the country to go forward under the aegis of the aristocracy to fulfil its proper role in Europe: to defend its own interests, like any other state, and to stand along with all others whose independence or liberties were threatened by the overwhelming power and aggression of Louis XIV. William III's heroic career had held up, but not permanently averted, the threat to Europe. At the time of his death, the accession of Spain and the Spanish Empire to Louis' grandson made Louis more powerful than ever before. The combined Bourbon power was necessarily Britain's chief antagonist throughout the high eighteenth century. At the beginning of the century, and until that power was reduced, there was the greatest danger of a French hegemony over all western and central Europe, and Britain's security was threatened along with the rest.

Nor did the English as a people see the danger at once—as again and again in their history, notably with the German aggressions of the twentieth century. A peacefully-inclined, a too kindly and easygoing people, like the Anglo-Saxons of the tenth and eleventh centuries, they would not see the danger which the dying William III saw. Fortunately, as with the German invasion of Belgium in 1914 and of Czechoslovakia in 1939, Louis himself opened the eyes of the British people with his recognition of James II's son as king: a breach of treaty promises and a direct intervention in our internal affairs. This roused the country and enabled William before his death to re-form the Grand Alliance between Great Britain,

Holland, and the Empire, and to designate Marlborough his successor as its executive instrument, a man of equal diplomatic ability with himself and of far greater military genius, if he was not William's equal in political heroism. Queen Anne, James II's second daughter, succeeded: a woman of a plain intelligence, whose reign Marlborough made glorious by his victories and achievements. Like the Stuart she was, in the end she discarded him. 'Marlborough as a military strategist and a tactician, as a war statesman and war diplomatist, stands second to no Englishman in history. His powers resemble those of Chatham and Clive rolled into one.' In effect, for the purposes of the war, and so long as the war was actively prosecuted, he was the executive arm of the state.

France began the War of the Spanish Succession (1702-13) with far greater advantages in every respect, save that of sea power, than the Grand Alliance. Her armies were in occupation of Spain, Italy, Belgium—the strategic hub of Europe; and she had a powerful ally in Bavaria, in the heart of the Empire. Yet the Alliance proceeded to roll back the tide of French power, and in this process English control of the sea was decisive. Marlborough understood the art of combining land and sea operations, the way that military power interlocked with financial, commercial, maritime, better than any other leader of our destiny save Chatham. Our success in the great struggle with Louis XIV was ultimately due to Britain's growing resources in commerce, finance, at sea, while those of France were exhausted with the strain of half a century's efforts at world conquest.

From Holland, Marlborough lunged across Europe with his mixed army of English, Dutch, and Germans in 1704 in full pursuit of the French who were making for Vienna. With his greatest victory, at Blenheim, he saved Austria, conquered Bavaria, and administered a great blow to France's military prestige. Two years later he conquered the Spanish Netherlands with his victory at Ramillies (1706) and in 1708 he kept the French out of them at Oudenarde. His fourth great battle, Malplaquet (1709), opened the way to an assault on the French frontier fortresses and the invasion of France. It was the lowest point in the fortunes of Louis XIV and peace should have been made then. But owing to the obstinacy of the Whigs and the Dutch, who were holding out for still better terms, the opportunity was missed and the war dragged on.

Meanwhile, the capture of Gibraltar and Minorca gave us bases for sea power in the western Mediterranean; the former has remained in British possession through all the vicissitudes of war and peace since. But the attempt to impose an Austrian king upon Spain very properly failed against the resistance of the Spanish people. The New Englanders captured what became Nova Scotia at the end of the war; the Hudson Bay territory was recovered and Newfoundland brought completely under our sovereignty. So that British power was extended on both flanks of the French settlements in Canada.

At home the Revolution settlement left its conflicts and difficulties. The aristocracy had won, but it was divided into two camps: Whigs and Tories. The Tories roughly were the party of the lesser but more numerous country gentry; the Whigs the party of the great landed oligarchs, the Dissenters and moneyed men. The Whigs' hearts were in the war; so were their purses. They conducted it, and they did well out of it. They raised the loans, on which the land tax paid by the country gentry and excise by the consumer provided the interest. As the war went on, the Tories became increasingly in favor of confining our land operations, cutting down commitments, and concentrating on sea power. After 1709, when the Whigs missed the chance of making peace, the Tories became the peace party. The duality of the party system revealed this advantage: that when one party would not do what was in the interest of the nation, the other could be called in.

And so the Tories made the Peace of Utrecht (1713). It was a very common-sense treaty, based upon a recognition of the state of things established by the war. Spain was to have the king of her choice, though a Bourbon, and the Spanish Empire in America remained attached to the Crown. But the Spanish dependencies in Europe went to Austria: the threat of French domination of the Netherlands to the security of Great Britain was removed. It provided a stable equilibrium in Europe until the French Revolution upset it once more. Our maritime and commercial interests were safeguarded: the expansion of our territory in North America was recognized, and a small footing for trade in the Spanish monopoly of South America, which we had fought for since the days of Elizabeth, was at last obtained: a fruitful source of dispute until the end of Spanish rule in the time of Canning and the prevalence of free trade.

The conflict for power between parties was reflected in the religious sphere and bound up with the issue of the succession to the throne. Whigs and Tories played into each other's hands by their mutual intolerance. During their brief period of full power (1710-14) the Tories tried to take away from Dissenters the education of their children and secure a monopoly for the church. This measure was repealed on their fall, which had become 'a necessary pre-condition of religious freedom.' Another measure, which was not repealed for a century, that insisting upon the ownership of a landed estate as a qualification for sitting in Parliament, reveals not only the basis of political power at the time, but also perhaps a certain perennial bias for the countryside in English social life. Both parties had supported the Act of Settlement which assured the throne to the Protestant Hanoverian line. But the heart of the Tory party was with the Stuarts, and not merely their heart but an underlying sense of their interest; for they felt not un-

naturally that when the Hanoverians came over, it would be
the Whigs who would sit on the right hand on high. This inner conflict within the Tory party, numerically larger and
more representative of the countryside, accounts for the fever-
ishness, the bitterness of party strife during Anne's reign. At
the end of it the Tory party was completely broken by Boling-
broke's attempt to make terms with the Pretender. It shattered
the fortunes of the party for two generations. The game was
in the hands of the Whigs. A certain oligarchic calm descended upon English politics after so much tension.

But this very tension had been, as is its way, fruitful in the
realm of literature, in which the reign of Anne made a brilliant epoch. The freedom of political discussion meant a
wealth of periodicals and controversial writing. The new prose
style of the Restoration, direct, simple, flexible, reached its
apogee in those classics of periodical literature, Addison's
Spectator and Steele's *Tatler*. Poetry declined somewhat from
the baroque magnificence of Dryden, a parallel in its way to
the architecture of Wren, the ornament of Grinling Gibbons,
the painting of Thornhill, the music of Purcell; it became,
like the prose of the age, more conversational and sociable,
often delightful, like the verse of Gay and Prior—until indeed
the supremacy of Dryden was succeeded by that of the brilliant, the versatile Pope. (It is curious that both these poetic
legislators should have been Catholics.) The Restoration
drama achieved perfection with the wit, style, and elegance of
Congreve. At the same time Bentley, greatest of English schol-
ars, initiated a new era in scholarship with his more exact
critical method. Perhaps the greatest writers of the age were
those most closely connected with political controversy: on
the Tory side, Swift; on the Whig, Defoe. For each of these
men, in addition to a mass of other writing, wrote one masterpiece of world-wide fame which has borne his name into in-

numerable languages: *Gulliver's Travels,* that astonishing creation of misanthropy which has passed for a children's fable, and *Robinson Crusoe,* which is one.

George I and George II (1714-60) were Germans: their contribution to English history was a negative one, but none the less useful. Since neither of them spoke English, and neither was a man of much ability, the business of the state was conducted by the Cabinet without the advantage of their presence. The powers of the Crown in the formation of ministries, the dissolution of Parliament, in patronage, tended to pass to the Whig oligarchy. Whichever section could command a Parliamentary majority held power: this again increased the importance of Parliament, which under the rule of the aristocracy succeeded the monarchy as the central political institution of the state. Seats went up in value, as they became more unrepresentative. As against the parliamentary corruption characteristic of an oligarchical age, there is this to be said—that it enabled young men of ability to gain experience of governing and play their part in directing the counsels of the nation, when with democracy men are apt to arrive at power and responsibility too late. The younger Pitt was Prime Minister at twenty-four: we have had few Prime Ministers to whom this country owes more; Charles James Fox was a Secretary of State at twenty-three: we have had few more distinguished. The Parliaments of the eighteenth century were corrupt, but they served the country no worse than the Parliaments of the past twenty years.

Out of these circumstances developed the Cabinet system as the instrument of government, by which the executive, with a good deal of managing on its part, was rendered ultimately answerable to Parliament. This, with its correlative development of the office of Prime Minister, has been called the 'essential part of the modern British polity.' It was the long

rule of Sir Robert Walpole that established these developments (1721-42).

Though high policy was in the hands of the Whig oligarchy
and their allies, the mercantile interests of the City, government could not be directed *against* the interests of the squire-
archy who were mainly Tory. And in fact the privileged position of the church was retained as an effective ideological basis
for rule: the alliance between squire and parson worked satisfactorily in the country, when the country was still overwhelm-
ingly dominant in English social life. Whig rule secured the
liberties of Englishmen, and thereby looked to the future,
because theirs was a minority party and they could not afford
to persecute. Two things distinguished Britain from the Continent: parliamentary control, freedom of speech, press, and
person. Even in this aristocratic age, class barriers were not
absolute; there was great social flexibility and a surprising
number of persons of humble origin made their way by ability
and patronage into society. Reason and moderation were its
keynotes; its intellectual mentors, Hume and Gibbon. Even
the case for Christianity was grounded by the great Bishop
Butler upon its reasonableness. Perhaps a degree of cynicism,
after so much ardor of conviction and of contradictory truths,
was what the country needed.

This it certainly got from Walpole, whose long period of
rule epitomized all these tendencies. The Hanoverian succession was attended with some difficulties. In 1715 the Highlands broke out in open rebellion. In 1720 came the crash of
the South Sea Bubble: a mania of speculation which swept
through society and was probably due to the over-confidence
engendered by the increase of trade and prosperity consequent
upon peace. Walpole, who had cannily made a fortune out of
South Sea stock, which went into building a vast country man-
sion and a collection of pictures (subsequently bought by
Catherine the Great and now in the Hermitage), was called

in to pull the country out of the mess; which he did very successfully. Peace and prosperity were not merely his aims, but his foibles. His tactics were never to raise issues which might disturb the internal equilibrium of the country: one great advantage of peace was that he did not have to increase the land tax upon the country gentry and so give the Tories a chance of re-forming their broken party. Two decades of this regimen served the country very well: trade progressed by leaps and bounds, and undoubtedly the fundamental resources of the country in commerce and finance were strengthened. But politically and morally it was lowering, and Walpole carried it too far. His policy of appeasement at all costs enabled the Bourbons to renew their aggression on the Continent and overseas. It needed a Pitt to call a halt to this.

In 1739 a dispute over the trading monopoly with Spanish America involved us in war not only with Spain but with France: a common Bourbon front was established. Pitt constituted himself the trumpet of the national spirit against that danger for the rest of his life. As usually happens in a war in which England engages after a long period of peace, she was ill-prepared and did badly at first. Combined operations in the West Indies and on the Spanish Main were ill-conducted and unsuccessful. At Fontenoy (1745) we were defeated, though the British infantry fought well. The same year another Highland Rebellion on behalf of the Stuarts brought the rebels as far south as Derby and panicked the capital, so low had public spirit been brought by the long peace of Walpole. After its defeat, it was necessary not only to subdue the Highlands but to bring them into submission. They were brought under Lowland law; their tribal chiefs were made landowners, their surplus tribesmen emigrated or were recruited into the army; military roads were run into their fastnesses, forts erected. It was the end of the problem and the last Stuart attempt.

After the war the French resumed the offensive overseas; a new spirit informed their imperial policy. In India the brilliant Dupleix conceived the idea of building up an empire in the south and, in conjunction with the native powers, driving the East India Company out. If he had not been met by the genius of the young Clive, he might have succeeded. In Canada the French planned a chain of military posts from the St. Lawrence to the mouth of the Mississippi, cutting off the English colonies from the unexplored west. In 1753 they drove the English traders out of the Ohio valley, and built Fort Duquesne to keep them out.

In these circumstances the struggle with France was renewed and again things went badly at the beginning. The Whig oligarchy was bungling its job. A new spirit, a new man, was needed. He came, not of the aristocracy, but of the new moneyed class: a man mad with pride, imperiousness, genius: William Pitt. An impossible colleague, he was an inspired leader: the greatest war minister this country has ever had. 'I know that I can save my country and that no one else can,' he said. And he did.

In two years of tremendous effort in which he directed everything, saw to everything, he won the war and harvested the fruits of his world-wide strategy. His plan was to keep France occupied in Europe by giving every support to Frederick of Prussia, while combined operations overseas isolated and overwhelmed her outposts of empire. He inspired the operations himself and chose the right men to execute them. In 1758 a combined land and sea operation captured Louisbourg, the key to French Canada. Next year Wolfe took Quebec, while the Highlanders and the American colonists drove the French out of the Ohio valley. Fort Duquesne became Pittsburg. French power in North America came to an end. 'The unexplored West was the Great Commoner's present to the English-speaking race.' In that same year of victories, 1759, Hawke's victory in Quiberon Bay, in which the French fleet was destroyed, recovered naval supremacy for the duration of the war. Meanwhile in India an empire had been founded by Clive's victory at Plassey and the assumption of direct rule over Bengal.

In 1760 George II died and was succeeded by his grandson, George III, young, ignorant, obstinate, anxious to govern and unfit to do so. Eager to recover the independence and authority of the Crown, he favored the Tories as a counter-balance to the Whigs. After so long a tenure of power the Whig oligarchy had split into a number of personal factions: a dangerous degree of disintegration which was increased by the personal action of the new King and by the intransigence of the great Pitt himself, who treated his aristocratic colleagues with more than aristocratic hauteur. He foresaw the proximate coalition of the two Bourbon powers, France and Spain, and wanted to strike first before Spain entered the war. The King wanted peace and intrigued for it against Pitt's ally, Frederick. Pitt resigned; Spain entered the war: he had been right. But by the momentum he had given to its conduct England continued to achieve successes against France in Germany, against Spain in the West Indies and the Philippines.

Peace was made in 1763. It was a far more moderate peace than might have been expected from the triumphs and conquests of the war. Havana and Manila were restored to Spain; a number of West Indian islands and commercial stations in India to France. But nothing could upset the main achievements of the war: the end of French power in Canada, the foundation of our empire in India. With North America under our rule, the Peace of Paris marked the apogee of British power and of the First Empire. It was indeed too great a predominance that had been achieved. Hitherto, for centuries, the security of the British state had lain in the fact that it was not so strong as to challenge the security and independence of others; hence it was the natural focus, owing to its geographical position and character, of coalitions against those states which were too strong and bent upon domination. Now, after the Seven Years' War, Great Britain had become such a power herself; and it was only natural that the continental powers, led by France and Spain, should seek an opportunity to band together and redress the balance. It was a dangerous pitch of exaltation that British power had reached after 1763, for herself and for others; the war had left grave problems of adjustment within the Empire; we were left without a friend on the Continent.

Such a moment demanded the highest powers of statesmanship. In fact, the disintegration of the Whig oligarchy brought about chaos in internal politics; this played into the hands of the King, who worsened the situation by his personal intervention in government. The one great statesman of vision and imagination who might have piloted the country through was incapacitated, exhausted by his efforts in the war, under a cloud of depression verging upon madness. For more than a decade things went on in this fashion: the affairs of a great empire were the sport not merely of party politics, but of personal faction, which raged to an extreme degree and reduced public spirit to a febrile condition. There were numerous changes of government; the country was run by a lot of second-rate men. They even neglected the navy, upon which our security rested; by 1778 it was inadequate to meet the demands made upon it; 'nothing had been done to remove the patent danger to an imperial country vulnerable in every quarter of the globe, of relying on an army and military system improvised in the hour of need.' At the end of those years of disgrace we had lost the North American colonies.

The termination of French power in North America had rendered the retention of the imperial tie less necessary. At the same time it provided the occasion for dispute. For the war had left a heavy burden of debt, and the home government was anxious to obtain a contribution from the colonies. The latter did not like paying taxes and refused to pay any that were not levied by themselves. That raised the constitutional issue, for though they had constitutional means of levying themselves, they were unwilling to band together to do so; they were only willing to band together to refuse. It was out of opposition to the home government that the colonies achieved a degree of unity. A great man like Chatham was opposed to raising the constitutional issue: he sensed imaginatively what depths of conflict it would open up; he would rather forgo the taxes. But the smaller men who took his place would not give up the token right. It was not for the amount of money involved, which was infinitesimal for purposes of imperial defense, but for the principle of the thing. They passed the Stamp Act (1765), an exiguous duty upon legal documents, which was then repealed owing to the opposition in America. To assert the principle the government, though actually lightening the duty on tea, undertook to help the East India Company to import tea at a low price, but which all the same bore a duty. The reply was the famous, the too-famous, Boston tea-party (1773) when a cargo of dutiable tea was raided and thrown into the harbor.

It was inevitable that the Americans should have the reality of independence. Now that the danger from the French was removed they felt themselves increasingly an independent people, with their own interests and rights. They would not have been English if they had not. It was not for nothing that they were descendants of the men who had left home rather than submit to the Anglican tyranny of Charles I and Laud. They had a fine Puritan tradition of resistance in their veins, and the lead was taken by Massachusetts, where it was strongest. They had, too, sympathizers in this country, among them the

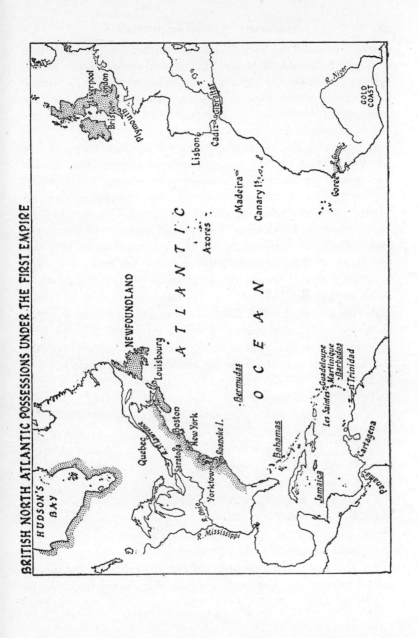

BRITISH NORTH ATLANTIC POSSESSIONS UNDER THE FIRST EMPIRE

greatest men of the age, Chatham, Burke, Fox; though not, it should be noted, Wesley. Political evolution was too immature to hit upon the right answer—self-government retaining the formal connection under the Crown—though Chatham seems to have glimpsed it. The Statute of Westminster of our own time would have met the case.

Behind this there was the economic conflict, the complex warp and woof of class sympathies and antagonisms. Under the prevailing ideas of the mercantile system, which ruled eighteenth-century thought everywhere, the colonies were regarded primarily as markets for the industrial products of the home country; restrictions were placed upon their commerce and industry in the interests of the export of those raw materials which the mother country needed. Necessary, and even beneficial, as this was in the early stages of colonial development, it became intolerable as the colonies reached economic maturity and demanded the management of their own affairs in their own interest. Economic maturity preceded, and helped to bring about, political maturity. It was inevitable that the colonies—they were the most advanced and self-sufficing of any in the world—should have their own way in these matters, and that, if they were not granted the substance of independence, there would come a breach, if not now, then later—probably in the course of the long struggle with the French Revolution and Napoleon. The pity of it was that owing to the obstinacy and lack of vision of George III's government, the breach should have come in the form it did.

Then, too, England was an aristocratic society, old, rich, hierarchical, while New England was a democratic community, independent-minded and egalitarian. The old country was on the whole conforming, socially obsequious: squire and parson ruled the roost; its tone and temper were hostile to, indeed contemptuous of, Puritanism, after the experiences of the seventeenth century. In New England Puritanism ruled, and with a very formidable temper.

The war, then, was genuinely, and tragically, a civil war. Sympathies were divided on both sides: many Englishmen were at heart with the Americans. If George III had won, he would have been able to impose a tyranny upon this country. In the colonies, a section of their upper classes, mercantile and professional men, landowners upon the coast, were loath to push matters to extremes and were genuinely attached to the connection with the old country. These were stronger in the Middle Colonies and the South than in New England. The radicals in America would not have been able to rally the conservative forces to their side if it had not been for the ineptitude of the home government's handling of the situation; the imposition of penal measures against Massachusetts, the closing of the port of Boston, mercantile and shipping capital of New England, brought about a united front among the colonists.

Even so, they might not have won their liberty if they had not produced a great leader in George Washington, a first-class soldier and organizer, a statesman of genius. A large Virginian landowner, his breeding and temperament were conservative and aristocratic, but he had a vision of the future of his country as an independent nation which bore him with infinite patience and fortitude through the trials and exasperations of the war. It is pleasant to think that this man who emerged as the victorious leader of a new-found nation came of oldest English stock, of a Durham family going far back into the Middle Ages; and it is right that his statue should stand now in Trafalgar Square along with Nelson and the worthies of the nation.

The military operations were as ill-conducted as the political: no Chatham now to supervise either; the great man was dying. (George III had denounced him as 'that great trumpet of sedition' and resented his burial in Westminster Abbey as a personal affront.) The first big campaign in the north broke down with the surrender at Saratoga (1777). That brought France and Spain in: the Bourbons saw their opportunity to reverse the decision of the Seven Years' War. What began as a revolt of the colonies ended as a war of Britain against half the world: the penalty we had to pay for the too dangerous ascendancy we enjoyed from 1763 to 1776. It was the one occasion in our history when the weight of a world coalition was brought to bear against us: we were defeated, and rightly; and thereby hangs a moral of the profoundest significance for our policy. To France and Spain was added the diplomatic and naval power of the Armed Neutrality of the North— Russia, Prussia, Holland, and the Scandinavian powers. Britain was reduced to straits indeed. The French fleet achieved the mastery in American waters in 1781, so that Cornwallis's army in the south was cut off by sea while it was blockaded on land by Washington. The surrender at Yorktown virtually ended the war in America.

'In the hour of need, to which her fools had brought her, Britain was saved by her heroes.' The thirteen colonies were lost, but Canada was saved. And after the war, numbers of loyalists who did not wish to break away from the Empire moved into Canada, forming a counterpoise to the French *habitants:* the twin foundation upon which modern Canada grew. The genius and tenacity of Warren Hastings saved British power in India at this crisis. Gibraltar held against the combined forces of France and Spain; and with the Battle of the Saints (1782) Rodney recovered the mastery of the seas against their fleets. Peace was made, upon a just foundation: the recognition of the independence of the United States. A new nation came into existence, a Republic under the presidency of her great leader, Washington, a people with a far greater future before them than the struggling seaboard colonies would have had still looking to the mother country.

The defeat was no less salutary at home: it ended the disastrous personal government of George III. It restored leadership to Parliament, the proper organ of political control, and to the men of ability within it. Two years after George III's defeat, power came into the hands of Chatham's son, another William Pitt, and for twenty-two years he remained the dominating figure in England's destiny. The defeat of the old régime opened a new and most hopeful era in the history of the Empire; soon the new Empire rivaled the old in its rapid growth and power, while its strains and problems were more satisfactorily treated under the influence of more liberal ideas.

Even in Ireland there was hope. That country had remained quiet throughout the century under the Protestant ascendancy; and under the influence of eighteenth-century ideas of reason, religious fanaticism on either side was at a low ebb. The victory of the Americans stirred Irishmen to demand self-government and freedom from external control: the lead was taken by Grattan, a statesman of vision, himself a Protestant landowner, and the movement had the support of Catholic opinion. For a brief moment of time Ireland was a united nation: her Parliament asserted legislative equality with the British Parliament under the Crown, and ended the commercial restrictions upon her exports imposed by English mercantile interests. Dublin was a capital: its splendid squares and public buildings reflected a brilliant and variegated social life. This was the Ireland that gave us Berkeley among philosophers, Goldsmith—whose *Vicar of Wakefield* had a European vogue—and Sheridan among writers; Burke and, later, Castlereagh and Wellesley among statesmen; among soldiers, Wellington. But the equilibrium was an insecure one, and it was broken by the violent impact of the French Revolution.

Rebellion (1798) brought about the imposed solution of the Act of Union (1801), which Pitt intended to implement and make real by enfranchising the Catholics. This George III refused: there ensued a century of misunderstanding, conflict, the growth of Irish nationalism, the struggle of a nation, ultimately successful, to be free.

Scotland meanwhile progressed by leaps and bounds. The Union with England was a great success: 'the mutual acceptance of each other by the two peoples has remained ever since one of the chief pillars of the British State.' Scottish agriculture prospered; industry made strides; the poverty of the country began to be left behind. The eighteenth century saw the hey-day of Scottish civilization. A 'New Town,' as magnificent as Bath, was added to the old Edinburgh, which became more of a social capital as it ceased to be a political. David Hume, profoundest and most contemporary in outlook of all British thinkers; Adam Smith, whose *Wealth of Nations* (1776) laid the foundation of modern economic thought and pointed the way to the new age in our industrial development: these men led the intellectual life of the whole country and exerted a European influence by their writings. The elegant and lovely painter, Allan Ramsay, and the more sentimental Raeburn, painted this world of Scottish fashion and intelligence; while the peasant poet of genius, Burns, penetrated into it, and the Shakespearean mind of Scott portrayed Scottish society and its past for all time.

In England profound agricultural changes, the discovery of new methods and technique, were changing the face of the landscape. It was now that the English countryside took on its familiar appearance, which strikes visitors from more spacious lands, of being parkland and garden. Jethro Tull started a new era in agriculture with his invention of the drill for sowing crops. Lord Townshend introduced and developed the cultivation of turnips and clover, making a new four-course rotation of crops possible, increasing largely the stock the land could carry and so producing richer crops again. Bakewell revolutionized graziers' methods, producing beef and mutton for the growing millions. Agricultural improvement became the passion, the hobby, the interest, of the great landlords, of whom Coke of Holkham was the champion, who by his introduction of new crops and artificial cattle foods multiplied the income from his estate by ten: a doughty opponent of George III in politics, the pride of his countryside, he set an example to the whole country. Arthur Young was the propagandist of the new agriculture, exerting an immense influence at home and abroad: English agriculture at this time led the world.

The old uneconomic system of open-field cultivation was swept away by an enclosure movement, at its height between 1760 and 1832, which touched all parts of the country: small-holdings were thrown together into larger; open fields were enclosed and divided up, waste spaces and commons swept into the improving possession of the landlord. The effects of this movement amounted to nothing less than an Agrarian Revolution, parallel to the Industrial Revolution now under way. In the first place, enclosure, along with the new techniques, enormously increased the productivity of the soil and enabled us to support a population which increased by half between 1750 and 1800, and doubled itself between 1800 and 1850. We were able to feed ourselves throughout the long twenty years' struggle with France. But the Agricultural Revolution riveted the control of landlord and capitalist farmer upon the land: it left a large class of landless laborers, a peculiarity of the English social system. Fortunately for them, the concurrent development of industry absorbed them, with some ups and downs of adjustment; so that a considerable internal migration from the country to the new industrial areas was an underlying feature of the new century.

Upon this basis English aristocratic society flourished. It was a very happy society for those who enjoyed it—and a great many did. It was the hey-day of a civilization that rested upon the country house. No country has such a wealth of them, small and great, dispersed through the length and breadth of the land. Eighteenth-century England was organized around them. It was the apogee of our domestic architecture, of English furniture and ornament, taste. Not that we were cut off from foreign influences; eighteenth-century society was very cosmopolitan in spirit. English artists were inspired by classical models, but they made out of them something of their own, a tradition more restrained, quieter, more moderate. One can see that this was so by comparing Wren's St. Paul's with Bramante's St. Peter's, or Gibbs's St. Martin-in-the-Fields with the churches of Rome or Vienna; or Georgian country houses with their models, Palladio's palaces. A succession of architects and designers gave the classical style an English idiom: Wren, Vanbrugh, Gibbs, Hawksmoor, Kent, the Adam brothers, Chippendale, Sheraton. The very landscape was designed, Kent and 'Capability' Brown and other gardeners exerting an influence upon the Continent as upon the face of our countryside. English painting for the first time achieved the dignity of a school: it was shaped by Italian and French influences, by the great figures of the Renaissance, the Dutch masters and Claude, but Hogarth, Reynolds, Gainsborough brought a charm, a sentiment of their own which was very English and expressive of the society they painted. Even in music, which was dominated by the gigantic figure of Handel after he settled in England, the movement was not all one way: native opera produced a masterpiece in *The Beggar's*

Opera, which had great influence upon the Continent; while church-music continued its tradition not unworthily.

It was above all in literature, the most characteristic expression of the English in art, that native genius flowered most richly and returned in its influence abroad something for the continuous inspiration which we had derived from Greece and Rome, Italy, France, and the Netherlands throughout the ages. Paris continued to be the capital of European civilization; but for the first time English thinkers, Locke, Newton, Hume, exercised as wide an influence abroad as at home. And not only philosophers either: the great novelist Richardson explored a new vein of sentiment which had its full flowering with Rousseau and Goethe's *Wilhelm Meister,* an influence which reached its term perhaps only with Proust. Sterne also belonged to this movement of feeling, the dawn of a modern self-awareness in literature. More masculine in genius were Fielding and Smollett, who gave us an unfading portrait, vigorous and realistic, of the coarse, energetic life of their time. Gray and Collins each wrote a few poems that are famous in our tradition: Wolfe said of the former's 'Elegy in a Country Churchyard' that he would rather have written that poem than take Quebec; and well he might. Cowper described the quieter side of the age, its domesticity, in his poetry and letters; Horace Walpole the world of fashion and power in his astonishing correspondence, a brilliant canvas. Dr. Johnson is perhaps its most characteristic literary figure: the subject of the greatest of English biographies, by James Boswell, a Scot. (Its only rival is by another, Lockhart's *Life of Sir Walter Scott.*)

The lawyer Blackstone in his *Commentaries* gave the most complete statement of English Law that had yet appeared: a model of classic proportion and style, the book had immense influence both here and in America. Among philosophers Mandeville and Butler were men of great originality, though on opposite sides over religion and morals; among scientists, Priestley, discoverer of oxygen, John Hunter, father of modern surgery. Of all the seamen of the age we can only mention Anson, who made a famous voyage round the world, and Captain Cook, greatest of Pacific explorers, who explored the coasts of Australia and New Zealand and discovered the Hawaiian Islands.

At home, evidence of a new stirring among the lower middle class and the people was the Methodist Movement. John Wesley was 'one of the greatest missionaries and the greatest religious organizers of all history.' As the result of his long lifetime of an almost Napoleonic energy and activity, a new religious community came into existence, with a contribution of its own to make to English life and an even greater future in the United States. Socially and politically conservative, it had the useful effect of keeping the lower orders quiet during the dangerously disturbed times of the French Revolution. At the same time it propagated a measure of popular self-discipline and built up a self-governing organization which had an influence, both directly and as a model, upon democratic political activity in the next century. Similarly, the Evangelical Movement had its effect in reviving ardor within the church. Its greatest triumph, one which affected the world, as well as political methods in this country, was its campaign for the abolition of the slave trade. In this its leader was William Wilberforce, friend of the younger Pitt. The campaign ran contrary to English economic interests, and very powerful vested interests were affected by it. Yet such was the ardor of conviction aroused that the slave trade was made illegal to British subjects in 1807, and slavery was extinguished throughout the British Empire in 1833, at the cost of a direct and outright payment of £20 million. Just in time, before the opening-up of Africa. It was a great deliverance for humanity at large. But for the West Indies, whose sugar plantations were dependent on slave labor, it meant economic ruin. In the eighteenth century perhaps the most prosperous of our colonies, today they are among the poorest.

George III's defeat meant a blessed interval for liberal policies before reaction closed in upon us with the struggle against the French Revolution. The Whigs put through half-measures of reform which made it impossible for Parliament to be bribed wholesale again as it had been ever since Walpole: henceforth it had to be managed. There was even some hope of electoral reform which would make Parliament less unrepresentative of the country; it had become increasingly more so throughout the century. The French Revolution postponed this till 1832. The loss of the American colonies meant that in imperial affairs the home government became more liberal, not less. In 1791 Pitt organized Canada into two provinces, Upper and Lower, corresponding to the geographical division and that between British and French population, and gave representative government to both. In India Pitt established the control of the home government over the political and administrative work of the East India Company: a settlement which lasted until 1858.

The outbreak of the French Revolution, which challenged the old order in Europe, deeply disturbed the harmony of classes that was characteristic of eighteenth-century England. A middle-class revolution, it offered hope of the future to all the popular elements which were excluded by the aristocracy from power. In its first idealistic phase it divided English opinion, and there was great sympathy with its aims and achievements among the middle and working classes. (The atmosphere of the time is rendered in *The Prelude* of Wordsworth, one of the greatest of modern poems.) The controversy over the Revolution gave rise to a body of distinguished political literature: on one side Burke, on the other Tom Paine and Godwin. At first Pitt refused to join with the reactionary powers in their attack on France; in 1792 he even lowered the strength of the army. But revolutions have a way of returning to national objectives reinforced with new vigor. And that same winter the Revolution burst the banks, carrying the tricolor where the lilies of Louis XIV had campaigned before: across the Rhineland and Savoy, into the Netherlands and threatening Holland.

It was a return to the old challenge to our security, along with the security and independence of others. That fundamental fact is the explanation of our long struggle with Revolutionary France and Napoleon, and of the successive coalitions with which Europe resisted their domination. So great were the energies released by the Revolution, so far-reaching its powers of organizing and inspiring a whole nation—and that with the greatest tradition in Europe as a civilizing power— so feeble was the popular appeal of the old monarchies, that it took Europe twenty years of struggle before the Continent was free once more. And then it was by the new national spirit aroused by the Revolution itself in the course of the struggle, among Spaniards, Germans, and Russians, in alliance with the ancient spirit of Britain. For England had an old tradition of its own: that, and her island security, the strong sea walls of her navy, gave her immunity and enabled her to hold out until the peoples of the Continent united in revolt.

Pitt was not an inspired war minister such as his father had been; he had not the flair for combined operations by land and sea: he was a man of peace. But he was a man of infinite courage, and a great political leader of a nation at war, an inspiration to Europe conquered but not defeated. He made mistakes, such as the deflection of our military forces to the West Indies, where they perished of disease, achieving nothing; other land operations were ill-prepared and ill-conducted. But Pitt's courage never failed at the worst moment of the war, when England's command of the sea was jeopardized by mutinies (1797). The very next year was the turning-point, when Nelson's great victory of the Nile rendered Napoleon's conquest of Egypt barren, made India secure, and recovered sea power in the Mediterranean, so enabling another coalition to take shape. The Peace of Amiens, which proved to be but a truce of a year (1802-3), left Napoleon dominant upon the Continent and England upon the seas.

The renewed war became a struggle of land power against sea power. Nelson's victory over the combined French and Spanish fleets off Trafalgar confirmed our security at sea: indeed it gave us security for a hundred years, during which our trade and commerce could advance peacefully in all parts of the world. Napoleon's victory at Austerlitz gave him the domination over central Europe. Nelson was dead; no one could foresee that his dominion would be more lasting. It was at this moment (1806) that Pitt died, at forty-six, worn out with the burden of office which he had carried since he was twenty-three; borne down by the cares and anxieties of the struggle. 'My country, how I leave my country!' he said when dying. His last speech to the nation had ended: 'Europe is not to be saved by any single man. England has saved herself by her exertions, and will, I trust, save Europe by her example.'

Napoleon tried to break the stalemate, and British resistance, with the organization of a Continental System, forbidding Europe to trade with Britain. Britain replied more effectually with the blockade of all Europe that submitted to Napoleon. The strain was great upon this country, where the working class suffered much hardship from unemployment and high prices, and it bore hardly upon the neutrals. The question was which would break first. To complete the extrusion of British goods from the Continent Napoleon was first led to intervene in Spain and then to make war on Rus-

ATLANTIC OCEAN

NORTH SEA

Scapa Flow

Jutland ✕

Copenhagen

Hamburg

Amsterdam

Bristol
London
Portsmouth
Sluys
Antwerp

Calais

Plymouth
La Hogue ✕
Cherbourg
Paris

Brest

Quiberon ✕

La Rochelle

Bordeaux

Corunna

Toulon

Rome

Barcelona

Naples

Madrid

Minorca

Lisbon

C. St Vincent

Cadiz
C. Trafalgar ✕
Gibraltar
Algiers

Malta

MEDITERRANEAN SEA

Miles
0   100   200   300   400   500

Naval Battles ✕   ○

Stanford, London.

sia: the first gave us our opportunity, the second ruined him. Britain sent an army to the Peninsula in support of the Spanish nation's revolt against Napoleon: together we saw to it that he was never free of the Spanish entanglement.

At the same time as Russia revolted against Napoleon's Continental System, the United States declared war upon Britain, in 1812. Various factors made for this unfortunate war: American feeling against the restrictions placed upon neutral commerce by the British blockade; their resentment at our exercise of the right of search. An aggressive element in the western and southern states wished to seize the occasion for the conquest of Canada and Florida; while New York and New England, which were most affected, were opposed to the war. The invasion of Canada was a failure; the British capture of Washington indecisive. In spite of gallant actions at sea by individual American ships, our stronger navy established its control of the coast. An American victory at New Orleans came after peace had already been signed, on the basis of the *status quo,* in 1815. In England the war was soon forgotten against the background of the great struggle with Napoleon. In America it was remembered, and for long remained an obstacle to complete understanding between us.

The Peninsular War (1808-14) restored the prestige of the British army, at a low ebb after the reverses of the earlier part of the war. Brilliantly led by Wellington, his small army from behind the lines of Torres Vedras, supported by Spanish guerillas, kept 300,000 French troops occupied and year by year inflicted mounting defeats upon them: Talavera, Salamanca, Vittoria. Meanwhile, the Continent was stirring behind the barrier. Napoleon's disastrous invasion of Russia and retreat from Moscow opened the floodgates of revolt. A coalition of European peoples, in which Britain, which had remained constant through all the years of adversity, took a leading part, overwhelmed him and his Continental System.

Nor was it disbanded when Napoleon returned from Elba to try his luck once more: it was Wellington in person, with a British army as the core of his forces, that defeated him at Waterloo.

In these circumstances it was not unnatural that the Anglo-Irish aristocrats, Castlereagh and Wellington, representatives of their class and country, should have had a decisive voice at the Congress of Vienna which settled the affairs of Europe after two decades of war. In agreement with Russia, but against the Prussian desire for revenge, they insisted upon a moderate, and even lenient, treatment of France. France kept her pre-war boundaries, retaining Alsace-Lorraine and receiving back from England most of the overseas possessions she had lost. British security was provided for by setting up a United Kingdom of the Netherlands, to which we restored Java and the Dutch East Indies. The Cape of Good Hope, Mauritius, and Ceylon we retained as strategic outposts of our growing Eastern Empire. (In 1819, through the far-seeing efforts of Sir Stamford Raffles, we acquired the site of Singapore, which later became the capital of the rich colonies that grew up in Malaya: the island developed into one of the great ports of the world.) In the Mediterranean we kept Malta, and the Ionian Islands, which were later made over to the Greek people. The Treaty of Vienna gave Europe a settlement that lasted for forty years. Its chief defect was that it did not give sufficient scope to the new forces of nationalism, which, in alliance with Britain, had brought Napoleon to an end.

The long and arduous struggle of the war did not exhaust the creative energies of the country. Indeed it saw the birth of a new literary movement destined to exert greater influence in Europe than any in our history—the Romantic Movement. The figures that had most influence abroad were Scott and Byron. But Englishmen think Wordsworth a profounder genius than either, and place him only after Shakespeare and Milton among their poets. His closest associate was Coleridge. In the next generation of Romantic poets came Byron, Shelley, Keats. William Blake, a mystic, a pure poet and admirable painter and draughtsman, went his own independent way, portraying his visions equally well by pen and pencil. So too in prose Jane Austen followed her own path, the perfect artist of the English novel. Among prose writers, the brilliant essayists, Hazlitt and Lamb, Southey the biographer, left work that lives. A galaxy of able writers on political economy, the philosophy of law and politics, initiated a new movement in thought and prepared the way for the next age to follow: notably Malthus and Ricardo among economists, and Jeremy Bentham, founder of the Utilitarian school of radicals.

In painting, the new Romantic inspiration reached its highest achievement with the work of Constable and Turner, the former of whom influenced French painting in turn; in portraiture Romney and Lawrence, who painted the notabilities of Europe assembled at Vienna. Two men of genius, Humphry Davy and Faraday, by their discoveries and inventions notably in chemistry and physics, laid the foundation for the immense expansion of the new era in scientific knowledge. Both were fortunate in the practical application of their work, particularly Davy, whose safety-lamp saved the lives of thousands of miners and whose *Elements of Agricultural Chemistry* performed a great service to agriculture by codifying the mass of chemical knowledge applicable to it. Their work in pure science went hand in hand with, and was part of, the immense expansion of science which underlay the Industrial Revolution.

The war had borne hardly upon the people. Where the landed classes and the investor throve on it, on increased prices and bounties on corn, on interest upon loans, the new manufacturing class and the agricultural laborers suffered much from unemployment, the ups and downs of trade, the steep rise in the cost of living, the indirect taxation which fell chiefly upon them. It was the concurrent fact of the Industrial Revolution gathering momentum all through the war that enabled the country to survive and come through it successfully.

VI. The Industrial Revolution

THE latest age in our history, that roughly covering the nineteenth century, is its most creative. It is not the one which English people regard with the greatest affection—that will always be the Elizabethan, which has for us the attraction of the heroic, the dew of dawn upon it. Perhaps the nineteenth century is too near for us to appreciate it: we are still part of the unceasing flood of economic and social change which it set in being, which brought with it such achievements in the material sphere, changing the face of the land, creating vast industrial districts across the countryside, multiplying the population two or three times, giving English society its contemporary form and the place in the world which we hold today. Its consequence is now, with a population of over forty millions in this small island, what Huskisson warned us it would be in the early stages of the flood, a matter of life or death for us as a nation: 'England cannot afford to be little. She must be what she is, or nothing.'

For good or ill—and it has the vastest potentialities for both —modern industrial civilization is the creation of this island: it is our chief contribution to world history.

The fact that the Industrial Revolution came about on our soil meant that though we profited enormously by being first in the field, we were also in some sense the victims of it. The storms and stresses, the problems it presented in the social sphere, were tremendous; it is probable that there were some spiritual losses, as there certainly were aesthetic, compared with the simpler, more natural and congenial society of our country-bred forefathers. But if there were losses, the chal-

lenge which so far-reaching a process of change presented w;
infinitely stimulating to courage and inventive energy; and o
the whole the way it was met was a triumph for our people.

The Victorian Age was an age of success. But it could neve
have had such success, surmounted such problems of adjus
ment, if it had not also been a period of unprecedented peac
That was due to the security, the unchallenged position at se;
which we had won as the result of the long war, our last, wit
France. There were small wars, or campaigns, on the frontie1
of the Empire, and one on the confines of Europe in which w
were engaged. But, on the whole, the reign of Victoria wa
one long peace in which the English people gave itself a
never before to industry and trade, work and money-making
the consequent export of surplus capital which helped to re
make the face of the world.

The political history of the country in this period is ther
largely a process of constant change, of reform and adaptation
in response to the pressure coming from new social and economic conditions set in being by the Industrial Revolution.
In the outer world it sees, naturally enough, considering the
surplus energy generated at home, not only a constant expansion of the Empire, but an increasing contribution of both
capital and labor to the development of new countries outside, notably North and South America. From European
affairs there was a certain withdrawal, a degree of isolation
which was only possible because of our supremacy at sea. Behind this security the country concentrated on its work, on
its own institutions, its own affairs. Never was there a period
when we were less influenced from abroad: the influence was
all the other way. It was as if the many centuries during which
we had absorbed foreign influences had come to fruition, and
this was now our age, in which to make the contribution most
characteristic of ourselves. In the end, such isolation, such a
withdrawal from Europe became dangerous, for after all we

are part and parcel of Europe, the point at which Europe is most in contact with the outer world. We cannot escape the logic of our historic position: the Victorian Age was a very exceptional period in our history; it has taken us now two world wars to make us realize how exceptional it was.

What, then, was the Industrial Revolution?

It is always difficult enough to define a revolution; but in this case the essence of the matter was the application of mechanical power to industry, constantly accelerating production, with all its consequences in transforming older social forms and bringing into being forces not only in the economic sphere but throughout society. This process gathered such speed by the beginning of the nineteenth century as to merit the name of a revolution; nor is it yet at an end: we are still involved in it and we have not yet succeeded in bringing these new forces under political control: hence the pains and penalties of our world.

The application of mechanical power to industry has a long history. In the seventeenth century there were several inventions of importance for the future; then came Newcomen's engine which made a partial use of steam-pressure and was in operation for pumping water out of mines. The invention of the steam-engine proper by Watt in 1765 was the cardinal event in the process. It made use of coal as the source of power. England was rich in coal, in close proximity to iron deposits; the application of coal to iron-smelting, at a time when our timber resources were becoming depleted, became the leading characteristic of the next phase of the Industrial Revolution. It meant the making of the Black Country, a new industrial district in the west midlands: the foundation of heavy industry. In forty years the output of iron increased ten-fold. Some idea of what the developments in this field alone meant for the country may be gained from this consideration—

at the beginning of the century England was behind other
countries in the working of metals, except for tin; by the end
of the century she was ahead of them all.

Simultaneously with this the application of mechanical
power was transforming the textile industries. As in the case
of the steam-engine, the search for improvement and invention
had been going on all through the eighteenth century; but
from about 1767 there came three cardinal inventions which
were ultimately to transform the industry: they were all concerned with cotton and all the work of Lancashire men: Har-
greaves, who invented the spinning-jenny; Arkwright, the
water-frame; Crompton, who combined the two in the 'mule.'
The transition from hand to steam power via water power
greatly influenced the location of the industry: it was concentrated wholly in Lancashire, a new industrial area. These
mechanical inventions were transferred to the Yorkshire
woolen industry; where in turn they attracted the industry
away from its older centers in East Anglia and the west country. For the first time since Anglo-Saxon days the north was
coming to rival London and the southeast in importance, a
shift in the equilibrium of the country which was to have increasing political consequence: in the demand for Parliamentary Reform, the enfranchisement of the middle class, the campaign for Free Trade. Those cardinal figures in the new age,
Huskisson, Peel, Gladstone, came from this area.

Along with this early phase in the development of industry
a revolution in transport was set in being, the end of which
is not yet. It was the first notable departure in speeding up
communications since the Roman era. So important, and characteristic, were these developments that some writers interpret
the Industrial Revolution in terms of their successive phases.
First came the canals, which knit together the industrial districts, particularly the midlands and the northwest. Then
came the new coach roads with their 'macadamized' surfaces,

which made much speedier traveling possible. Next came the Railway Age, which more than anything else brought the country together as one unit, with its communications pivoting upon London. The later nineteenth century saw the prodigious development of the steamship and of steamship routes across the oceans. The mass-production of steel which came at the same time and which we owe to the inventions of three Englishmen (one of them a German naturalized), Bessemer, Siemens, Gilchrist Thomas, gave us a long lead over other countries in steel production, something like a monopoly in shipbuilding and in the mercantile marine. The twentieth century has seen the development of the motor-car, which has brought the road system back into service, and the airplane, which has annihilated distance and revolutionized the conditions of power alike at sea and on land. All this has been the harvest—and the inspiration—of the labors of many men of genius and ability: Brindley, Rennie, and Telford, builders of canals, roads, bridges, lighthouses; Trevithick, who first made a steam-locomotive; engineers like the Stephensons, the Brunels, Armstrong, Sir Charles Parsons, inventor of the steam-turbine; projectors like Hudson the Railway King; shipbuilders like Napier and Palmer; inventors like Dunlop and a host of others.

Impossible to do justice to such a torrent of creative energy, such variety of achievement: the potteries of Staffordshire in which the Wedgwoods played such an important part, uniting art with science and industry; the copper and brass industries of Birmingham; the linen manufacture and shipbuilding of Belfast and Glasgow; the coal and tin-plate of South Wales; the shipbuilding, steel, and chemicals of the northeast coast. All that we can say is that we hear a new rhythm in our history, the thud and beat of hammer and steam-pistons, and recognize the face of modern Britain. So different from the England of the Edwards and Henries and Elizabeth, of

Marlborough and the Pitts—and yet with so much that is continuous and recognizably the same in the character of the people.

There were many predisposing factors which made it inevitable, when one looks back, that the Industrial Revolution should have come about first in this country. It was rich both in coal, the new source of power, and in iron; industrial communications were easier than in any other country. Then, too, England was already the first commercial and maritime country of the world: the trade outlets were already there for our exports, an expanding internal market for imports. This meant that there was a high degree of skill among artisans, from which the new inventions profited. Above all, it meant that there were surpluses of capital to invest in them and in the processes of production they gave rise to. It may well be that we owe the Industrial Revolution to the fertilizing influence of capital more than to any other factor, and among the makers of our later history we must include the great capitalists.

The effect of these profound changes was to break up the harmony of the old social order, to bring new classes into being, and create the antagonism between capital and labor characteristic of modern society. But there can be no doubt about the fundamental achievement of the Industrial Revolution: an immense increase in productivity which has enabled a far larger population to support itself on a much higher standard of living. It is this more than anything that accounts for the prodigious increase in the population during the reign of George III from seven millions to fourteen; by the end of the nineteenth century it was nearly forty millions. And this in spite of a large emigration to the United States, and another stream which helped to people Canada, Australia, New Zealand, South Africa in the course of the century.

There was often great hardship, unemployment, want, over-

THE INDUSTRIAL REVOLUTION

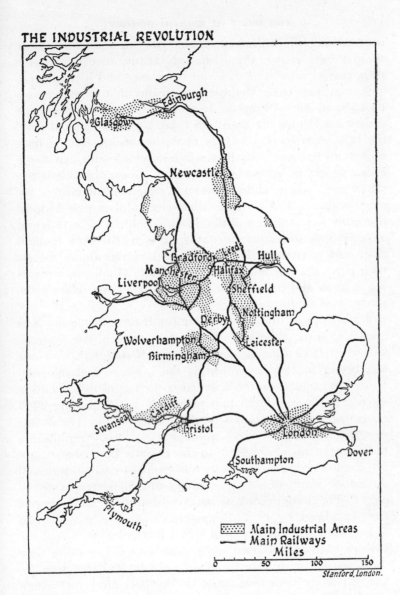

Edinburgh

Glasgow

Newcastle

Bradford Leeds Hull
Manchester Halifax
Liverpool Sheffield
Derby Nottingham
Wolverhampton Leicester
Birmingham

Swansea Cardiff
Bristol London
Southampton Dover

Plymouth

░░░ Main Industrial Areas
— Main Railways
Miles

0   50   100   150

Stanford, London.

work among the industrial masses. But we hear much more about these things in the nineteenth century precisely because there was a quickening of social conscience and higher standards were expected. Men were conscious that it was, exceptionally, an Age of Progress. In all earlier times the life of the great mass of men has been very hard. Now, for the first time, the expansion of productivity made it possible for the bulk of men to live out their lives without actual want. An astonishing variety of institutions came into being to provide better conditions—benefit clubs, insurance societies, committees for social welfare. The churches themselves took a new lease of life with new responsibilities in this field; a new religious organization, the Salvation Army, was created by a remarkable leader, General Booth, and had extraordinary success with its work. The activities of the Trade Unions in organizing sickness and unemployment benefit were even more widespread and important.

We are apt to think of the nineteenth century too much as an age of *laissez-faire*. Even before the process of freeing trade from the restrictions of mercantilism was complete, the state had begun its task of protecting the workers, and the community at large, from the worst consequences of industrialism. A code of factory legislation was built up, beginning effectively with the Factory Act of 1833, and the Ten Hours Bill of 1847, limiting hours of work and eventually prohibiting the employment of children. In this crusade Lord Shaftesbury was the leader. An inspectorate was created to watch over conditions of work, of safety in mines and dangerous employments. The long record of surveys of public health begins with Chadwick's epoch-making Report of 1844: his was one of the formative influences of the century, the creator of the modern code of sanitation and public health. The slums were the worst legacy of the Industrial Revolution: the price we had to pay for its coming about first in this country. The state was slowest in grappling with the enormous problem of re-housing the people; and in spite of Royal Commissions, and the activity of various trusts, it was not until after the last war that real progress was made. Meanwhile an elaborate system of public health services had been built up, which reached its culmination with the creation of the Ministry of Health (1918). The effect of all these activities has been a spectacular decline in the rate of mortality, an achievement in which we led the way, until it has become one of the lowest in Europe.

In short: the story of the nineteenth century is on the political side a process of constant change and adaptation of institutions to new conditions, while the gradual creation of social services by both voluntary and state effort was its grand contribution to social welfare.

The long struggle with the French Revolution, and the fear that it aroused among the propertied classes, unnaturally prolonged the Tory monopoly of power and postponed political reform till 1832. Until then the landowners ruled the country, with on the whole the support of the middle classes. There was a great deal of unemployment and unrest among both industrial and agricultural workers after the war. Food prices were high; the agricultural interests took their opportunity to pass a Corn Law (1815), putting heavy duties on the import of corn and so keeping the internal market to themselves. In these years were the first beginnings of the modern working-class movement in politics. Its chief propagandist was the voluminous and admirable writer, William Cobbett. But a more fertile influence was ultimately that of Robert Owen, who after a career as a model factory-owner took to the propaganda of socialist ideas, encouraged the growth of early Trade Unions, and was the inspiration of the Co-operative Movement. An interesting parallel with the French St. Simon: it is significant that socialism should have been the creation of the two most advanced countries in western Europe.

Behind the façade of Tory rule, the strain between land-owners and the middle class was becoming apparent; the political history of the mid-nineteenth century is largely concerned with the latter's struggle for independence. The Tories were driven to make concessions; and indeed a new liberal Toryism was forming, more in keeping with the new tendencies of the time, under Canning and Huskisson. In 1824 Pitt's Combination Acts, which had prohibited the formation of Trade Unions, were repealed. Huskisson progressively abolished a large number of duties, and went a long way in the direction of Free Trade; the landowners would not, however, consent to free imports of corn.

Canning was the moving spirit of the new Toryism, which meant, rather, liberalism in foreign policy, encouraging the struggle of smaller nations for their liberty and independence, as against the aristocratic spirit of Castlereagh, who wished to preserve the Congress of Vienna settlement of Europe in line with Metternich. The Congress system had become increasingly reactionary; and when the powers intervened in Spain to extinguish a liberal régime and restore the Bourbons, Canning took the opportunity to recognize the independence of the revolted South American colonies. He was determined that whatever might happen in Europe, the Reaction should not get a hold in the New World: the meaning of the famous phrase that he had 'called in the New World to redress the balance of the Old.'

The emancipation of Latin America was one of the decisive movements out of which the political system of the modern world has come. In this complex struggle covering a whole continent, from which a number of new and vigorous states emerged in the course of a single generation, a dominating role among the powers was played by Britain. Her naval power and trading interests gave her a position which she used to safeguard the nascent states from European intervention. Castlereagh was sympathetic to their independence; but it was Canning's greatest and most enduring work to hold the ring for them diplomatically until they had established their right to exist, and then to set the seal upon it by British recognition, which other powers were forced to follow. In this course of policy, executed with the greatest skill, he was supported by the liberal sympathies of the middle class, the commercial interests of the City of London, and the new humanitarian movement. Our countrymen provided far the most numerous contingent of those who fought alongside the South Americans: the fleets of Brazil and Argentina were organized and led by British officers, the staff of the great Bolívar, the Liberator, was largely manned by English, Scots, Irish. Canning's diplomatic efforts served both their interests and ours. Independence ended the long struggle with Spain over restrictions upon colonial trade; the new countries needed both cheap imports and capital investment, which the progress of the Industrial Revolution was enabling Britain to provide.

Before he died, Canning was on his way to a victory upon the continent of Europe: he was largely responsible for the independence of Greece. Byron was the hero of the Greek cause in the public mind, but it was Canning who made it politically possible—and against the sympathies of Wellington and Castlereagh, who were pro-Turk and disliked revolutionary movements anywhere.

The pressure of circumstances was too much for the old Toryism. After Canning's death, his opponents, Wellington and Peel, were forced into making two concessions that marked a great breach with the historic past. The Test Act, which had kept Catholics and Nonconformists out of office in state and municipality ever since Charles II's time, was repealed; and, still more surprising, Catholic Emancipation, which was withheld at the time of the Act of Union, was conceded to Ireland. It was a capitulation to the demand of O'Connell, leader of the Irish people.

In England the campaign for Parliamentary Reform was in full swing; at moments it looked as if it might boil over into revolution—as in France in 1830. But in the end the governing class gave way, and the Reform Bill was passed in 1832. By this only one-half of the middle class was enfranchised, and none of the working class. It was a very great departure all the same: the rotten boroughs were abolished, seats redistributed, giving much fairer representation to the new large towns, industrial areas, and the counties. Even more important: it pointed the way to further reform, a process which went steadily on for the rest of the century, instead of revolution followed by reaction. It was a great crisis well turned. The Reform ministry carried a variety of measures and then sank back exhausted. It put through a national reorganization of the Poor Law, which stopped the pauperization of the laborer—at the cost of great severity; and it reformed local government in the towns by giving all ratepayers the vote. But it is worth remarking that the countryside remained subject to the squires. In that dualism lies much of the subsequent history of our parties: the country the stronghold of Conservatism, the towns of Liberalism, and later of Labour.

The 'hungry 'forties' were a period of much distress and agitation: harvests failed, the price of corn soared, there was much unemployment and dislocation, a railway boom and a collapse, budget deficits. The 'condition-of-England question' came into the forefront of discussion and is reflected in the literature of the time: Carlyle's *Chartism,* the earlier novels of Dickens, *Oliver Twist* and *Hard Times,* Disraeli's *Sybil: or the Two Nations.* It was in reality the growing-pains of the new industrialism; but people did not know that then and wondered whether they were not permanently debilitating.

The working classes were up in arms against the ills of their lot, the harshness of the New Poor Law, the denial of any share in parliamentary representation to them. Various streams of agitation, from London, the Midlands, South Wales, the North, coalesced into a movement behind the People's Charter, demanding a share in political power for the working class. It was premature by half a century or more.

Chartism was a real challenge to the existing order. In France a similar movement led to the Revolution of 1848: that gave the signal for revolutions all over the Continent. In England the governing classes met the challenge by a judicious mixture of firmness and concession. Peel was the pilot who rode out the storm. Enormously wealthy, the son of a Lancashire factory-owner interested in factory legislation, educated at Eton and Christ Church, Peel represented in himself the junction of the old world and the new. It may not have been congenial, but it was very powerful; it was above all immensely public-spirited, incorruptible. He is said to have been the last English Prime Minister to have a command of the detailed administration of every department. Earlier he had been responsible for creating the police force—called after him 'bobbies' or 'peelers': a step of the greatest importance in maintaining public order by civilian methods. Now (1841-6) he restored order to the state's finances by a series of masterly budgets: lowering many duties on imports and at the same time reducing deficits by reintroducing Pitt's income tax. Starting his political life as a die-hard Tory, Peel had reached the point at which he thought of politics in a non-party way in the interest of good administration and the country. He was making towards complete Free Trade. The test was to be the repeal of the Corn Laws.

A rival agitation to Chartism took the field under middle-class leadership—the Anti-Corn Law League of Cobden and Bright. For some time it had been gaining increasing hold upon public opinion. But the disastrous Irish potato famine of 1845-6 forced Peel's hand. The Irish population, which had doubled itself along with the English, was now some eight millions—and Ireland had had no Industrial Revolution to support it: they lived on potatoes. That year hundreds of thousands starved; still more fled from the stricken country— to Britain, Australia, Canada, above all to America. It was the turning of the ways in Irish history. Peel decided to ignore the basis of his party's support and to abolish the corn duties. Disraeli led a revolt of the Tory landowners against his leader, which succeeded in breaking him at the height of his power. The Repeal of the Corn Laws was the most important event of mid-Victorian politics, for it broke the Tory party and kept it out of power for a quarter of a century. Its ablest younger leaders, notably Gladstone, passed over into association with the Liberals. The middle class had won a great victory over the gentry, the industrial interest over the agricultural. It remained to follow up its logic, and the new political methods the League had developed, into other fields. With the 'fifties prosperity returned; nor did the Repeal of the Corn Laws harm agriculture: it shared the increasing prosperity of the time.

The heir to Canning's foreign policy was Palmerston. Everywhere abroad he was in sympathy with liberal movements; these sympathies, shared by Gladstone, were consistently exerted in support of Cavour and the movement for the creation of a United Italy. In the crisis of 1859-60 out of which the new Italian kingdom emerged, Palmerston's support was decisive: as with Canning over Greece, he made the birth of the new nation diplomatically possible. His liberal policy abroad brought him into direct conflict with Tsarist Russia under the reactionary Nicholas I: out of which the unfortunate Crimean War arose, our only war with Russia throughout our history. One good result of this otherwise regrettable episode was that it brought us into association with France; another, that it showed up aristocratic incompetence in the army command and in administration. The real hero of the war was Florence Nightingale, who performed a miracle in bringing down the rate of mortality in war hospitals by introducing modern methods of hygiene and nursing. An indomitable woman, an organizer of genius, she was a precursor of the twentieth century: for she was an ardent feminist and supported John Stuart Mill's campaign for Women's Rights in politics and the professions.

Palmerston was a consistent supporter of the cause of Polish independence. He protested strongly against Austria's annexation of Cracow in 1848; at the end of his life, over the national rising of 1863, he attempted to intercede again for the Poles. But the alliance between the three reactionary Eastern Powers was too strong for him. Again, his sympathies were wholly with Denmark in the campaign which Bismarck planned against her; but he was unable to help her, for Bismarck was determined upon war, which the profoundly peaceful Victorians were unwilling to resort to. It was true, as Bismarck said, that Palmerston's policy was mere bluff; but even a poor bluff was a more civilized thing than Bismarck's blood and iron, as Europe was to prove. The civilized powers of the West, England and France, had to confess defeat for the first, and not the last, time at the hands of German aggression. Its full importance was not realized at the time by an England bent upon the arts of peace, industry, and commerce. It led straight to the defeat of France in 1870. Even so it was long before we learned the lesson: that we must stand together or perish separately. The defeat in which Palmerston's career ended increased English aversion to taking a part in European affairs. That cleared the way for Bismarck. It was in fact profoundly symptomatic of the new age abroad: the comfortable Victorians had not taken the gauge of the militarism of modern Germany, applying all the prodigious powers of industry and science to a barbarian tradition of war and a systematic purpose of aggression.

The leading English figure of the age was Gladstone—whom Bismarck could not abide. A deeply religious man, a strong Churchman, a follower of Peel (also, like him, Lancashire and Oxford), Gladstone, who had started as a Tory, became every year more liberal and ended up in extreme old age an advanced radical, looking forward into the twentieth century. During the American Civil War his sympathies, like those of the English governing class in general, were with the South. The working classes, in spite of the hardships the war entailed upon the cotton-spinning area, were whole-heartedly with the North. The issue of the war had its effect upon English internal politics: it encouraged democratic opinion and added to the demand for political enfranchisement of the working class. This was partly met by Disraeli's Reform Bill of 1867, which gave the vote to all householders in the towns. Gladstone carried the process further in 1884 by enfranchising the agricultural laborer and miner—household suffrage in the counties.

The enfranchised working class gave Gladstone the support for his famous ministry of 1868-74, in which he accomplished his chief work of adapting the old institutions of the state to the needs of a more democratic age, creating new ones where necessary, but preserving the best in the spirit of the old. Determined to rid the bureaucracy of the incompetence and favoritism shown up by the Crimean War, he boldly applied the examination system of the old universities to qualify for entrance to the civil service. It has had a profound effect upon the country, in helping to form an administrative class impregnated with public spirit, admittedly incorruptible, and far better equipped for the work of a modern state. In 1870 a national system of elementary education was created—somewhat belatedly, owing to the mutual jealousy of the religious

sects. The coping-stone was placed upon this with the creation
of a national system of secondary education in 1902. The old
universities were reformed by Royal Commissions. An important series of army reforms was carried through, upon which
the modern military system was founded.

So great was the new impulse for reform that it was continued by Disraeli's Conservative Government (1874-80); and
not unwillingly on his part. Disraeli's service to his party—
after the great disservice he did by breaking Peel—was to bring
Conservatism up to date, to make terms with the new democracy. This he did in two ways: by his sympathy with working-
class legislation, and by a certain feeling for the Empire. He
gave the Trade Unions legal security, made an attack on the
slums with his Artisans' Dwelling Act, and tackled public
health. All this with the gay banter of an old phrase-making
buccaneer: 'Sanitas sanitatum,' he had said, 'omnia sanitas.'
In foreign policy he was a strong supporter of Turkish power
against the advance of Russia into the Balkans. Gladstone's
sympathies were with the smaller peoples, Bulgars, Greeks,
Southern Slavs, who had been submerged but were now ex-
periencing the stirrings of nationhood. At the Congress of
Berlin in 1878, Disraeli held up the Russian advance, but by
'backing the wrong horse,' supporting the decaying Turkish
Empire instead of the vigorous young Balkan peoples. His
purchase of the Suez Canal shares strengthened our connection
with Egypt, indispensable from its situation on the route to
India and the Far East. Queen Victoria, with whom his relations were conducted in terms of almost Elizabethan homage
and gallantry, he made Empress of India. Mr. Gladstone, who
'addressed her like a public meeting,' was less successful both
with her and with the Empire. A liberal, gravitating towards
radicalism, he was deeply opposed to any spirit of expansion-
ist imperialism and anxious for the extension of self-government. The genuine conflict of personality and conviction be-

tween these two great men filled the stage of Victorian politics for the average Englishman.

In the background the beginnings of a new political movement destined to be of increasing importance in the nation's life were to be discerned. The 'eighties witnessed a new spirit, an outburst of activity in the working-class and Trade Union movement. A great dock strike in 1889 led to the 'New Unionism'—the organization of large masses of unskilled workers into Trade Unions. A small but brilliant circle, Sidney and Beatrice Webb, Bernard Shaw, and others, formed the Fabian Society for discussing and working out measures of practical socialism. In the next half-century the Fabians exercised an influence upon public life, particularly in regard to the development of social services, poor law, the institutions of government, welfare economics, upon the Trade Unions, within the civil service itself—an influence that is comparable only to that of the Utilitarians earlier in the century. William Morris, poet and artist, and others started various organizations for the propagation of socialism. The tradition started by Owen, which had been dropped in the 'fifties, experienced a revival. His co-operative ideas had been successful in the field of distribution: the Co-operative Movement grew larger every year. A new phase in English domestic politics opened when certain of these socialist organizations joined with the Trade Unions to form a new independent political party (1900): the Labour party. In its organization from the beginning the leading parts were taken by Ramsay MacDonald and Arthur Henderson. With the election of 1905 the new party first became a group in the House of Commons, a factor in politics. It was destined in time to succeed the Liberal party as one of the two leading parties in the state.

In these circumstances of complete security at sea plus the tremendous industrial development going on at home, export

of goods, capital, expansion of markets, there was an extraordinary, though perfectly natural, growth of the Empire
abroad. It must not be forgotten that, in addition, the surplus
energies of the country—capital equipment, mechanical skill,
emigrants—played a great part in the industrial development
of countries outside the Empire. Notably in constructing the
railroads of the United States, which opened up the virgin
prairie and made possible the shipments of wheat which from
the later 'seventies began to depress, and transform, British
agriculture. British engineers and skilled workmen had also
had a share in building the railways of the Continent, as again
later in South America, in the Near and Far East.

But we are concerned here with the evolution of the Empire itself, of which the most significant feature is the progress
of self-government within it; in this Canada led the way. Its
apostles were Lord Durham and Gibbon Wakefield. Durham
was both an imperialist and a radical. Sent out to investigate
the agitation which had broken out into a rising in 1837, he
recommended that complete responsible government as at
home should be granted at once 'freely and trustingly.' That
famous Report laid down the guiding principles in the new
phase of the Empire's development. Durham was a follower
of Gibbon Wakefield, who believed that the grant of self-government with the subsequent reciprocity of interest would
mean that 'Britain would become the center of the most ex-
tensive, the most civilized, and above all the happiest empire
of the world.' In Canada the provinces were re-united under
one legislature; in 1867 a further step was taken when the
provinces, which had increased in number and population
with the opening-up of the west, voluntarily formed a federa-
tion, restoring autonomy to French Canada. The achievement
of nationhood by Canada aided the working-out of a peaceable
settlement of the boundary with the United States in the
course of the century. In this it has formed a primary link

in the friendship between the British Empire and the United States, which, signalized by alliance in two world wars, is a determining factor in the history of our time.

The example of Canada has been followed in the case of other colonies as they became ripe for self-government. The colonization of Australia and New Zealand was undertaken more deliberately by the home Government, seeking to recoup itself in the southern hemisphere for the loss of the American colonies. The Australian colonies were separated from each other by greater distances and a more straggling economic development; it was not until 1901 that they achieved their Federal Union. The chief contribution of Australia and New Zealand has been in the examples they have given of progressive social legislation.

South Africa has had a far more complex and exciting, a too exciting, story: the triangular situation between Dutch, English, and Africans has been the source of its troubles—and also of its interest. These led to a series of small wars in the century, culminating in the Boer War of 1899-1902. With the development of the Rand gold mines, bringing the Boer hinterland into the forefront of world economic advance, it was impossible for two small agrarian republics to hold aloof from the general movement in South Africa. All around them the powers were staking out their claims. In that economic advance the leading part was played by a financier of vision, Cecil Rhodes, who looked to the expansion of South Africa northwards into the territories now known as Rhodesia, and nursed an imperial project of a direct route from the Cape to Cairo under British control.

It was inevitable that South Africa should be unified within the British Empire rather than outside it; it was a tragedy that owing to impatience on one side, obstinacy on the other, the way should have been through war. But all Englishmen are proud of the fact that four years from its conclusion a

Liberal Government, which had been in no way responsible for the war, carried Durham's principle of granting self-government 'freely and trustingly' into action. In 1908-9 these same Governments came together to form the Union of South Africa; and for its entire history it has been governed by men —Botha, Hertzog, Smuts—who fought us in 1899-1902. Of the leadership and vision of Smuts, not merely in South Africa or within the Commonwealth, but in world affairs, no member of that Commonwealth, of whatever race or nationality, can be too proud.

The truth is that the British Empire has been turning itself into a Commonwealth of Nations, united in a common allegiance while at the same time governing themselves. In this evolution, which achieved statutory form with the Statute of Westminster of 1931, the Dominions played the leading part. Britain has become the first and oldest of the Dominions. So far from thinking this a loss, we regard it as a logical development of our history; and the Commonwealth itself, a practical and working example of a League of Nations, as perhaps the chief contribution in the realm of political organization which we have to make to this age.

In India the break-up of the Mogul Empire and the success of British arms and administration in that welter of conflicting races, religions, and states left British power paramount. Inevitably, and whether we wished it or not, government was forced to extend its scope and area: it was the one organizing center that remained. A succession of great administrators, Munro, Metcalfe, Elphinstone, Dalhousie, built up an astonishing structure of government in a short time. But the process was perhaps pushed too fast by the Governors-General, partly as the result of wars with the predatory, military races in which they became involved. It was too radical for the age-long conservatism of Indian society; the reaction came with the Mutiny of 1857. This was a deeply disturbing experience;

it created a legend for Anglo-Indians, the deeds of Nicholson and the Lawrences, Havelock and Colin Campbell, the relief of Lucknow; but it severed something in the earlier easier relations between the two peoples. After it the government of India was taken over from the East India Company by the Crown. It developed ever further the beneficent work of building railways, irrigation, famine relief, health services; and there can be no doubt of its marvelous achievement when one considers that a population of perhaps a hundred millions has risen to nearly four hundred millions during the British Raj. In our time the problem has become as with Canada a century ago that of handing over government to Indians themselves: a problem immensely more complicated because of the divisions within the country and the difficult legacy of the past.

A problem of similar complexity, if on a smaller scale, was that of Ireland, which dominated home politics in the later nineteenth century. Gladstone devoted the last phase of his extraordinary career to finding a solution which was in keeping with the wishes of the Irish people: Home Rule. He was before his time; he was defeated by the obstruction of the House of Lords and the obstinacy of the Unionists. He initiated land legislation to assure Irish tenants fair rents and security of tenure: a process which was completed later by buying out the Anglo-Irish landlords—a reversal of several centuries' history. The proper coping-stone of this was the grant of self-government, as elsewhere in the Empire. It was a tragedy that Gladstone was defeated, largely by the defection of a wing of his party under the leadership of Joseph Chamberlain. It meant for Ireland the postponement of her legitimate claims, the embittering of internal conflict, until they were only conceded as the result of a national rebellion, with all its deplorable consequences in mutual distrust and memories of suffering.

For England the consequences were no less harmful. The

Liberal party was split and out of power for twenty years. The long rule of Lord Salisbury left little that was constructive in social legislation. Its chief advantage was that his cool wisdom tided over the diplomatic conflicts attendant upon the partition of Africa; and in administration its chief importance lay in the Colonial Secretaryship of Joseph Chamberlain (1895-1903).

The opening-up of the interior of Africa had been mainly due in the first place to British explorers: Mungo Park, Lander, Livingstone, Speke, Stanley. In commercial development, too, and in missionary effort Britain had taken the lead, both in West and in East Africa. At the same time she had been anxious—it was a continuous thread running through her colonial policy—not to increase her liabilities by political annexation. From 1884 onwards, however, there came a change, with the entry of Germany into the colonial field. Bismarck pushed and blackmailed; Gladstone and Salisbury were conciliatory, and in the end wide concessions were made in West, South-West, and East Africa to the newest colonial power by the oldest. But as a result of this 'Scramble for Africa,' in which Britain was forced to defend her economic and strategic interests by formally annexing territories where her influence had long been paramount, she became possessed, still with reluctance, of a vast new empire.

It was Chamberlain who first among British politicians sensed the full potentialities of the tropical colonies, in Malaya as well as in Africa. By his reform of the Colonial Office, his far-reaching constructive plans of economic development, and the assistance he gave to research (notably in following up Ross's momentous discovery of the cause of malaria, made in 1897), he laid the foundations for the later prosperity of the dependent Empire. In administration and methods of government a parallel development began in Chamberlain's day; and with the theory of 'indirect rule'—associated espe-

cially with the name of Lord Lugard, one of the greatest of
our colonial administrators—Britain has made a characteristic
and striking contribution to modern colonial practice.

In spite of the deplorable spirit growing up in the new Germany, one of aggressiveness, a combination of envy and blustering, English policy was not unfriendly to her. At the turn
of the century, conscious of isolation at the time of the Boer
War, Chamberlain made approaches for an understanding.
They were never reciprocated: the fact was that Germany was
determined to become a world power, not only dominant on
the Continent but capable of challenging Britain at sea. That
was a matter of life or death for this country.

English opinion would always have preferred an understanding with our own kith and kin of the United States; and
towards the end of the century, when they were involved in
war, our sympathies witnessed to the decided change of sentiment in this country towards America consequent upon our
own transition from aristocratic to democratic government.
But we understood the difficulty under their constitution of
their making any hard-and-fast alliance. It was essential for us,
in entering upon the twentieth century, with other powers
catching us up in the industrial field while surpassing us in
military strength, to end the political isolation which reflected
the exceptional security for us of the nineteenth century. This
meant a return to an earlier, sounder tradition: to our historic
role of allying ourselves with all other powers threatened by
the aggressive spirit and intention of one—in the modern
world, Germany. We began with an alliance with Japan,
which in those early years had the advantage of protecting
China from partition among the European powers. We went
on to an *entente* with France, which cleared up all outstand-
ing issues between us. It was completed by an understanding
with Russia, which similarly settled matters long in dispute.

Our relations with Italy had always been friendly. Great Britain, face to face with the growing challenge of Germany at sea, as others were on land, was no longer isolated. Nor were they—as they had been kept in Bismarck's time.

This immensely significant reversal of policy, or rather return to our historic tradition, was set in train by a Conservative Government; it was completed by a Liberal ministry, during Sir Edward Grey's long tenure of the Foreign Office. The reaction against two decades of Conservative rule came in 1905 with an immense Liberal majority, which, mainly through the administrative impulse of Lloyd George and Winston Churchill, pushed through big measures of social reform. Of these the biggest was a national scheme of sickness and unemployment insurance. Other measures were defeated by the House of Lords. There was a prolonged constitutional crisis, the most serious since 1832, with two elections in 1910. From this the Lords emerged with most of their powers shorn by the Parliament Act of 1911. But the prolonged deadlock and deflection of energy into constitutional channels slowed down the pace of social legislation, had its effect in industrial unrest, and re-awakened the Home Rule question in its acutest form. And meanwhile all the activity of this Government—one of the ablest in our history—was overshadowed by the menace of Germany. Germany had tried out her now familiar methods of aggression to test the strength of the Anglo-French *entente* in two diplomatic crises, Tangier and Agadir: the bond held. Her challenge to our very existence grew with the building of a great High Seas Fleet. Our internal troubles, constitutional and industrial, over Ireland, over female suffrage, strikes, were moving to a crisis in 1914 when Germany let war loose on Europe.

One cannot write the history of the First World War in a paragraph; it is enough to say that we can appreciate its nature and origin a good deal better now in looking back from the experience of World War II. No one can now doubt that the prime cause of it was the insatiable desire of Germany for power, to impose her domination upon others. And that accounts for the fact that she had to encounter a coalition of all who felt themselves threatened. This proved her undoing, as it was of Philip II, Louis XIV, Napoleon. In that world coalition Britain played a pivotal role. The burden of the war fell mainly upon France, Russia, Britain. On land we bore our part chiefly upon the familiar pitch of Belgium and northeastern France, as well as upon other fronts, in Italy, the Dardanelles, Palestine, Mesopotamia, East Africa. There were a million British dead. But the most vital front of all was at sea; it was the relentless pressure of sea power that more than anything brought German aggression to a halt, as it had Napoleon. Nevertheless, so great was Germany's strength that she held the world at bay for four years, and then only collapsed when the illimitable power of the United States began to make itself felt.

After four and a half years of untold suffering and destruction a moderate treaty was imposed upon Germany at Versailles (1919)—of an undeserved moderation compared with what Germany would have imposed had she been able, of which indeed we have evidence in the treaties of Brest-Litovsk (1918) and Bucharest (1918). Having lost the war, Germany proceeded to organize sympathy. She never really attempted to fulfil the conditions of the Treaty—a patent insincerity which provoked the French into their occupation of the Ruhr (1923). The world-wide success of her campaign to place all blame for her discontents and the troubles of Europe upon the Treaty of Versailles was the first and greatest example of her prowess in propaganda, of which we have had many since.

The structure of world peace designed by the Treaty, the effectiveness of the League of Nations, was indeed deranged by the withdrawal of the United States into isolation and the reluctance of Great Britain to undertake responsibilities on the Continent. Britain in the post-war period was affected by the example of the United States; she was drawn to closer contact with her Dominions in the outside world; she had many troubles of her own, financial, industrial, social, problems of maladjustment consequent upon the war, of changing trends of trade, chronic unemployment; she wished to disinterest herself in the problems of Europe, if only it were possible, and to return to the security and ease of the nineteenth century. But it was not possible; this was the twentieth century; the nineteenth was a very exceptional interval in our long story. So strong, however, was its hold upon Englishmen's minds that they went on under the illusion that it was possible. They did not see that the withdrawal of ourselves and the United States from the continent of Europe upset its proper equilibrium and opened the way for Germany to profit by it to make a second and even more dangerous bid for world-power. The lesson we have had to learn in a renewal of suffering; we are in Europe and of it, and we cannot escape our responsibilities towards it.

In these post-war years at home much was done to alleviate the ills created by the earlier industrialism; an effective campaign against slums was launched, and a rehousing of a considerable part of the population was carried through by the local authorities aided by the state. Educational facilities were greatly improved; unemployment insurance extended, old-age pensions increased; public health and social services vastly advanced. The state was in process of turning itself into a welfare state; and certainly that is a better ideal than that of a power state. All this was the better side of its activities in the post-war period. The country suffered in its public life during those decades from the loss of so many of its young men in the war, who would have come to the fore had they lived. But it did not even make proper use of the men of transcendent ability who piloted the state through the war, men in the tradition of Marlborough, the Pitts, Canning: Lloyd George and Winston Churchill. It preferred to turn to mediocre men, whose names shall not be mentioned in this history, though they may not be forgotten.

A historian cannot but feel a deep satisfaction that at such a fateful moment as the present the nation has found a leader of uttermost courage, whose vision is rooted in a historic sense of our past and the exigencies our position imposes upon us: one who on one side of his stock goes back to the great Marlborough who saved England and Europe from the aggression of Louis XIV, and on the other to descendants of English stock in the thirteen colonies which became the United States, eldest daughter of the mother country.

Of the immense creativeness of the past century we have given some idea in some spheres of culture; it is impossible to do justice in all. We may say that it was particularly rich in science and literature, as was to be expected of a society governed by a continuous Industrial Revolution with all the rich variety of its effects in social change, its ups and downs. The latter we should expect to afford favorable soil for the development of the novel. And so it was: the Victorian Age was the hey-day of English fiction. In Dickens it had its greatest master, whose influence upon the Continent was only less than Scott's. (It was particularly strong upon the Russian writers.) His novels, in their infinite invention and inexhaustible humor, provide a portrait of a whole society: the 'lower orders' of the Victorians, especially the lower middle class to which Dickens belonged. Thackeray painted, with irony rather than with any love, the upper middle and professional class. Trollope described the life of the gentry with convincing realism; the Brontës and George Eliot—the best artist of them all—the life of the countryside, its comedy and tragedy, its poetic power. Two novelists who at the same time were poets brought the Victorian tradition to a close: Meredith and Hardy, the latter one of our greatest. H. G. Wells and many others continued the aftermath of the tradition; but a new impulse came only in our own time with novelists whose work approximated to the condition of poetry: Joyce, Virginia Woolf, D. H. Lawrence.

The age had its representative poet in Tennyson, the laureate of the Victorians, superb craftsman and artist, a magician in words, a belated Merlin. Later Victorians found themselves more faithfully mirrored in Browning; the strain of the age, the breakdown of the older certainty movingly expressed in Arnold; the note of rebellion and defiance in Swinburne. Poets and artists like William Morris and Rossetti reacted against the commercialism of the time and turned back to the Middle Ages for inspiration. The Victorians had their prophets, like Carlyle and Ruskin, to whom they allotted an importance out of proportion to their aesthetic value. Carlyle was the leading representative of a German influence in thought, which was largely, if not wholly, deplorable. The influence of German philosophical idealism did not come to fruition until the end of the century, with Bradley and Green, when it for a time overlaid the sounder tradition of English empiricism which came to a stop with John Stuart Mill. He was the most representative thinker of the time, and a profoundly sympathetic one: the Locke of the Victorians. A man of freedom and immense toleration, deeply impregnated with liberal ideas of society and the ultimate value of human personality, in touch with the best French thought, he was also sympathetic to socialism. After Mill, economics was given a new direction by the work of Alfred Marshall, whose mind may be said to have dominated the modern approach to that science. The influence of German scholarship in theology and history was more beneficial, though here too we had our own older tradition, which culminated in the work of the Cambridge theologians, Westcott, Hort, Lightfoot, and of Colenso, also famous for his single-minded championship of the Zulus in South Africa. Oxford produced Newman, among divines: perhaps the greatest prose-writer of the century. Then there were great historians, a goodly company of them: Macaulay, Grote, J. R. Green, Stubbs, Froude, Maitland, the finest scholar of them all. On the borderland between the humanities and science comes the new discipline of anthropology, which Tylor did most to shape. Its greatest ornament was the work of a mind which has more deeply influenced our outlook than perhaps any other: James George Frazer, author of *The Golden Bough*. An influence comparable to Freud, he taught us the relativity of institutions and beliefs.

In pure science Darwin by his work on Evolution gave his name to an epoch: it is possible that no English scientist, save only Newton, has had such an influence upon the world's thought. Something of this prodigious influence was due to the masterly propaganda of T. H. Huxley, and to the systematic reduction of the idea of the 'survival of the fittest' to an extreme individualism by Herbert Spencer. For all that, Faraday is the scientist's man of science with his instinct for the way Nature works, his natural genius as experimenter, investigator, expositor. Clerk Maxwell carried Faraday's work on electromagnetism a further stage, to a revolutionary synthesis. Joule and Kelvin made great advances in studying the transformation of forces and forming the doctrine of energy, 'the central doctrine of nineteenth-century physical science.' Perkin first discovered aniline dye, so founding a vast industry, and may be regarded as the founder of the industry of coal-tar products. Ramsay, Lord Rayleigh, Rutherford, J. J. Thomson developed a whole new field of investigation into radio-active substances and the structure of atoms. Lister was the creator of antiseptic surgery, whose contribution to science and humanity closely fits in with that of Pasteur. These are perhaps the greatest and best-known names—and there are still great men omitted; the number of lesser workers in the field is legion. For the nineteenth century was nothing if not a scientific age.

In the arts proper, in music, architecture, painting, it did not excel. The social transition of the time, the confusion of standards, the pushing commercialism of the middle class, the decline of aristocratic taste upon whose patronage these arts had depended, were conditions adverse to them. There was no painter of the first rank after Turner. The Pre-Raphaelite school was a provincial affair, whose best work was a by-product: its influence upon standards of internal decoration. In painting above all, the Victorians suffered from their lack of contact with the Continent; for France at that time was the scene of one of the greatest periods in the history of art. Not until that contact was renewed did English painters achieve great work: Whistler, an American born, who painted mostly in Paris and London, Sickert, Wilson Steer, Augustus John. Victorian architecture, after the Regency impulse had exhausted itself, exhibited a mingle-mangle of styles, much vulgarity, and, in general, deplorable taste. That state of affairs, too, began to improve with the new century and the work of Lutyens, a return to the sound and distinguished tradition of Wren and the reign of Queen Anne. In music also, after a long and almost inexplicable hiatus for a people who in earlier centuries had led Europe, there were the beginnings of a Renaissance. Elgar, a very English composer, gave most moving expression to the religious and emotional side of his people's nature: his countrymen feel it deeply in his work. Delius was more exotic in his inspiration, though he had indigenous sources; he lived much in France, an English parallel to the impressionism of Debussy. Vaughan Williams, happily still alive, has returned to the native soil of English folk-song and the golden age of the Elizabethans, and out of these twin inspirations has created a body of great work. As in painting, so in music, we are now in the midst of the second generation of a Renaissance after the discouraging interval of the Victorian Age.

In literature, always the most vigorous of the arts with us, there has been no cessation of activity. Wilde and Shaw, Synge and Barrie and Galsworthy brought about a rebirth of the drama which has been more prolific than at any time since the Restoration. An Anglo-Indian writer of genius, Kipling, an unquiet spirit, had a career of symbolic importance: among other things, he gave expression to the phase of rather blatant Imperialism about the turn of the century. Hardy, after a full-length career as a novelist, proved himself a great poet in his old age. Yeats, like Wilde and Shaw and George Moore, the novelist, was a recruit to our literature from Ireland: the most lofty and admired poet of his time. His successor in this eminence is a recruit from New England: T. S. Eliot. The creator of a small body of poetry himself, he has had an influence comparable to that of Coleridge in its effect upon the poets coming after him: the new school of poets, like those in music and painting which have emerged since the last war.

All told, these are evidences that there is no slackening in the creative impulse of our people and that the stock is sound. Nor is it ultimately to be counted against us that so much of our energy in recent years has been devoted to the arts of peace.

Epilogue

WE are now in a position to understand something of the leading traits in the long, and in a way strange, history of this country and its people. For there is something strange in the fate of the small island which, for so long on the outer fringe of the civilized world and held down by an alien governing class, has come to play in the end such an extraordinary part in world history.

Perhaps it is well that on the whole English people have been unconscious of the strangeness of their country's fate. It might have given them a sense of strain, the kind of inner tension which the Germans live under and which is the clue to much of their unhappy history. In fact there is no such strain with the English; they are an easy-going, kindly, tolerant folk: one can see something in them still of the same characteristics that exposed the Anglo-Saxons to the ruthless Normans. They have an instinctive sense of moderation, which one can observe in their history, and that perhaps has been their preservation, a clue to their success. There is a very common proverb on the lips of ordinary English people, *Live and let live,* which astonishingly expresses the spirit of their history when you reflect upon it. It is only at times and in places where they have departed from it that they have come upon disaster, with the American Colonies, in Ireland. But defeat itself was chastening and they learned to make concessions. They learned from the loss of the First Empire to concede self-government to colonies which had grown up to maturity. The governing class at home learned to make concessions to other classes as they grew in strength and sense of responsibility and demanded a share in power. And so, in spite of the unparalleled strain of the Industrial Revolution upon the people who first experienced it—and that in the course of a century which saw frequent outbreaks of revolution elsewhere —there was no revolution in this country, but a consistent evolution of self-government.

We owe much of the good fortune of our later history to our insularity, which has imposed a buffer between us and the shocks and impacts of great movements, whether military or social, coming from abroad. That has given us a chance in some measure to absorb them, to mold them to our own purposes, to work out our own solution of them in comparative peace and quietness. And so, in the fullness of time, after an apprenticeship to foreign influences, a course of preparation longer than that of any other European country, we have come since the Reformation to have some contribution of our own to offer to civilization in return for the immense debt which we owe, above all, to the Latin world. From that time it has been an expanding contribution until it reached full flower in the modern period, with the eighteenth and nineteenth centuries. No one can question its creative richness, vigor, variety—whether in political institutions or ideas, philosophical and religious toleration, personal freedom, in maritime and military achievement, in the realm of commerce and finance, in discovery and colonization, in the industrial changes which are the basis of modern civilization; or in literature, science, the arts.

The long record of English history has been fortunate beyond belief: the greater the duty that rests upon every Englishman to see that the future is not unworthy of the past.

Note on Books

THE reader will find the following books useful for studying English history in further detail. Quotations in the text are usually from one or other of these works.

G. M. Trevelyan: *A History of England.* 1937.

Logan Pearsall Smith: *The English Language.* 1912.

Sir W. J. Ashley: *The Economic Organisation of England.* 1914.

Sir Cyril Fox: *The Personality of Britain.* 1938.

R. G. Collingwood: *Roman Britain* (Oxford History of England). 1936.

R. H. Hodgkin: *A History of the Anglo-Saxons.* 1940.

F. M. Stenton: *William the Conqueror.* 1925.

F. M. Powicke: *Medieval England.* 1931.

H. A. L. Fisher: *History of England, 1485-1547* (Political History of England). 1906.

A. F. Pollard: *History of England, 1547-1603* (Political History of England). 1910.

J. A. Williamson: *The Ocean in English History.* 1941.

G. M. Trevelyan: *England under the Stuarts.* 1904.

Sir Charles Grant Robertson: *England under the Hanoverians* (Methuen's History of England). 1934.

C. R. Fay: *Great Britain from Adam Smith to the Present Day.* 1928.

R. C. K. Ensor: *England, 1870-1914* (Oxford History of England). 1936.

Basil Williams: *The British Empire.* 1928.

Eric A. Walker: *The British Empire.* 1943.

J. A. Williamson: *A Short History of British Expansion.* 1930.

R. W. Seton-Watson: *Britain in Europe, 1789-1914.* 1937.

The reader is recommended to consult *A Readers' Guide to British History*, by J. A. Williamson, which includes annotated suggestions of books for further reading, and *British History*, compiled by Professor A. S. Turberville, a select list of nearly two hundred books without annotations. These can be obtained from the National Book Council, 3 Henrietta Street, London, W.C.2.

British Book News, a classified and annotated list of new books in all subjects, including history, can be obtained free by residents outside the United Kingdom on application to the National Book Council.

THE BRITISH EMPIRE SHOWING THE DISTRIBUTION OF BRITISH MER-
CHANT SHIPPING OF 3,000 TONS AND OVER ON 24 NOVEMBER 1937

Chronology

EVENTS		GENERAL MOVEMENTS
B.C.		**A.D.**
55	Caesar's first invasion of Britain	—100
A.D.		—200 ⎱ Roman occupation of Britain
43	Roman Conquest begun	—300 ⎰
123	Completion of Hadrian's Wall	—400
		—500 ⎱ Saxon invasions
597	Augustine arrives in England	—600 ⎰
664	Synod of Whitby	—700
		—800 ⎱ 850-99 Alfred
		—900 ⎰ Danish invasions
		—1000 ⎰
1066	Battle of Hastings	⎱ Norman conquest 1066-87 William I
1086	Domesday Book	—1100
		⎱ Development of the Common Law 1154-89 Henry II
1170	Murder of Becket	
1215	Magna Carta	—1200 ⎰

1272-1307 Edward I

-1300 }Conquest of Wales

-1400 {Hundred Years' War

}Wars of the Roses

-1500 {Tudor monarchy

}Spanish war

-1600 Charles I's Personal Rule
{Civil War: reduction of Scotland and Ireland
1st Dutch war
Oliver Cromwell's Protectorate
2nd and 3rd Dutch wars

1688-1702 William III

-1700 }Wars against Louis XIV

1265 Simon de Montfort's Parliament
1295 Model Parliament

1314 Battle of Bannockburn
1340 Battle of Sluys
1346 Battle of Crecy
1348-50 Black Death
1381 Peasants' Revolt
1399 Deposition of Richard II
1415 Battle of Agincourt

1497 Cabot's 1st voyage

1529-35 Reformation Parliament
1535 Dissolution of the Monasteries begun
1584 1st English colony in America
1588 Spanish Armada
1600 East India Company chartered

1640 Long Parliament summoned
1649 Execution of Charles I
1660 Restoration of Charles II
1688 Revolution: accession of William III
1690 Battle of the Boyne
1692 Battle of La Hogue

1704 Battle of Blenheim
1707 Union of England and Scotland

General Movements

Ministry of Walpole
Wars against Spain and France
} Seven Years' War
} War of American Independence

—1800

Revolutionary and Napoleonic wars

American Civil War

—1900

Boer War
1st World War
2nd World War

Industrial Revolution

Events

1713	Peace of Utrecht
1745	Highland Rebellion
1763	Peace of Paris
1776	Declaration of American Independence
1783	Treaty of Versailles
1789	Outbreak of French Revolution
1801	Union of Great Britain and Ireland
1805	Battle of Trafalgar
1807	Prohibition of British slave trade
1815	Battle of Waterloo
1815	Treaty of Paris
1832	1st Reform Bill
1839	Durham Report
1846	Repeal of Corn Laws
1857	Indian Mutiny
1867	2nd Reform Bill
1884	3rd Reform Bill
1886	1st Home Rule Bill
1900	Formation of Labour Party
1904	*Entente* with France
1911	Parliament Act
1922	Establishment of Irish Free State
1931	Statute of Westminster
1939	Outbreak of 2nd World War

Index

DATE DUE

UUN 1 '66			
JAN 25 '67			
UUN 7 - '67			
MAY 4 '72			
APR 11 '74			
DEC 12 '74			
NOV 1 0 1977			
NOV 1 1 1983			
			PRINTED IN U.S.A.